THE HENRY M. JACKSON LECTURES
IN MODERN CHINESE STUDIES

# CHINA
## Asia's Next Economic Giant?

### DWIGHT H. PERKINS

UNIVERSITY OF WASHINGTON PRESS

*Seattle and London*

*Library of Congress Cataloging-in-Publication Data*

Perkins, Dwight Heald.
    China, Asia's next economic giant?

    (The Henry M. Jackson lectures in modern Chinese
studies)
    Bibliography:
    Includes index.
    1. China—Economic conditions—1976–  .  2. China—
Economic policy—1976–  .  3. East Asia—Economic
conditions.  I. Title.  II. Series.
    HC426.92.P47   1986      330.951′058       86-15786
    ISBN 0-295-96402-2

The Henry M. Jackson Foundation established the Henry M. Jackson Visiting Professorship in Modern Chinese Studies at the University of Washington in 1984. Few memorials could honor the interests and concerns of Senator Jackson more appropriately than support of Chinese studies at his alma mater.

Senator Jackson had a deep and abiding interest in China. During the last decade of his life he visited China four times, in 1974, 1978, 1979, and 1983. His influence on our nation's China policy during this critical decade would be difficult to overestimate. On each visit he met with the highest Chinese leaders and had wide-ranging discussions with them on foreign and domestic affairs. He did not content himself with conversations in Beijing, but allotted time for extensive travel in the country, visiting different regions as part of his effort to understand the historic problems the Chinese people faced in building a modern nation.

Senator Jackson viewed China with deep respect, both for its long-term contribution to human civilization and for its more recent achievements in attaining national unity. The Senator believed that our nation lacked an adequate understanding of China, that there was a national shortage of specialists with the requisite knowledge of Chinese language, culture, and history. He believed that the United States needed to base its future policy toward China on a sound understanding of Chinese society and institutions.

Accordingly, it was natural that the Jackson Foundation

should seek to memorialize this concern by establishing this Visiting Professorship in the Henry M. Jackson School of International Studies at the University of Washington. The Professorship is devoted to the study of modern economic, political, social, business, and legal conditions in China. Occupants of the Professorship will rotate to bring the world's leading experts to the Jackson School, where they will deliver public lectures, offer courses, and lead symposia for the benefit of the University, the Pacific Northwest community, and—through publication of the lectures—scholars and the general public throughout the world.

# Contents

# Preface

These two related essays are the written version of two lectures I delivered at the Jackson School of International Studies of the University of Washington in October 1985. The lectures inaugurated the Henry M. Jackson Visiting Professorship in Chinese Studies of that school.

After twenty years of studying about China, learning the Chinese language, and traveling around the periphery of China, I made my first trip to the People's Republic of China in 1974 in the company of Senator Jackson. I also accompanied the Senator on two of his other trips to China, in 1978 and 1979. Scoop Jackson played an important role in the normalization of relations with China and it was a privilege for me to play a bit part in his efforts to that end. But in many ways the most personally rewarding part of those trips to China was the opportunity to get to know and learn from Scoop. He had a remarkable grasp of how the American government works and the role that the United States was capable of playing on the international scene. He saw issues in historical perspective, and our breakfasts, lunches, and dinners frequently turned into seminars on contemporary American history in which he had been such a central figure. For these many reasons, it was a special pleasure for me to be given the opportunity to inaugurate the professorship named after him.

Many people worked to make these inaugural lectures a success, but I wish especially to thank Helen Jackson for her role with the Jackson Foundation in creating the chair, and

*Preface*

Kenneth Pyle and Nicholas Lardy of JSIS for all of their considerable efforts in making these lectures a success. Nick Lardy was also of help with comments on an earlier draft of the manuscript, and Gretchen O'Connor was responsible for the production of both the final version and the earlier draft.

DWIGHT H. PERKINS
Belmont, Massachusetts
March 1986

# 1

## *The East Asian Development Experience*

The rise of East Asia to a position of wealth and power is one of the major forces shaping the international economic and political system in the latter half of the twentieth century. Japan began its rise around the turn of the century, but then stumbled badly as domestic political upheaval led the nation into foreign adventures and the near total destruction of its cities in World War II. Between 1950 and 1980, however, Japanese gross national product rose fourteenfold to turn Japan into a giant economic power, surpassed only by the United States and, barely, the Soviet Union. The annual rates of growth of 9 and 10 percent that had fueled Japan's rapid rise were then matched in the 1960s and 1970s by South Korea, Taiwan, and the two city states of Hong Kong and Singapore. Between the early 1950s and the beginning of the 1980s, Taiwan's GNP rose eleven times and Korea's nearly eight. Taken together these four rapid developers had a population about half that of Japan. Growth in much of Southeast Asia, notably in Indonesia, Thailand, and Malaysia, also accelerated in the 1960s and 1970s, although not so rapidly as in the East Asian four.

It is an event of some historical significance when nearly 200 million people become a part of the industrialized world and leave behind peasant agriculture and the extreme forms of poverty that characterize peasant agricultural societies. How much more significant would it be if China, with more than a billion people, were to become an industrialized nation by the end of this century or shortly thereafter/ It took one hundred and fifty years for the industrial revolution to begin in England in the late eighteenth century and then sweep across the rest of Europe and North America, raising the living standards in an area that today encompasses roughly 700 million people (excluding the Soviet Union), about 17 percent of the world's total. If the Soviet Union is included, the number of people rises to 23 percent of the world's total.[1]

If China's efforts to become an industrialized nation succeed, then 1.1 billion more people will live in newly industrialized countries than was the case as late as the 1950s. In the course of four or five short decades, we will have moved from a world where the great majority, three quarters of the total, lived in poverty, mainly rural poverty, to a world where half of the people live in relatively prosperous, predominantly urban societies. Furthermore, because the East Asian nations, each in a different way, managed to eliminate the more extreme forms of income inequality, growth has benefited or will benefit the great majority of the people, not just a select few.

If the main beneficiaries of these developments are the people of East Asia themselves, they are not the only people influenced by what is occurring there. Rapid growth was accompanied and to some degree caused by even more rapid rates of increase in exports from East Asia. Industries in the West that compete with products from East Asia have faced stiff competition and the need to adjust quickly. Not all of them could do so, resulting in plant closings and unemployment in the United States and elsewhere. There has been much casual talk about the deindustrialization of America being caused by this international competition, but reality is not so melodramatic. Japan's share of total world export trade rose from 3.5 percent in 1963 to 6.5 percent in 1973 and 7.5 percent in 1983. The East Asian four plus China, taken together, followed closely behind, rising from 2.6 to 3.8 to 5.8 percent of total world trade over this same period. Thus East Asia's share of foreign trade has risen rapidly over the past two decades, but even in the early 1980s, 86 percent of all world exports were accounted for by nations not in East Asia. The real problem is that accelerated export expansion from East Asia has been concentrated in a few highly visible products (textiles, steel, televisions, and automobiles) and thus has had a large political impact that has helped undermine support for an open international economic system.

On the positive side, the economic success of East Asia derived from its open economic policies has influenced many nations to rethink how they ought to go about achieving economic development. In the 1950s and well into the 1960s, in contrast, involvement with the international economic system by developing countries was a necessary evil at best. The model of how to achieve rapid growth was the autarkic centrally planned Soviet Union. Both India and China were heavily influenced by perceived Soviet economic success. For Latin America the origin of import substitution strategies where nations attempt to grow by substituting domestic production for imports lay in its own political and intellectual traditions and its perceptions of the outside world, but the result was similar. Rapid growth could only be achieved by minimizing one's involvement with the economic systems of the United States and Europe.

South Korea and Taiwan may be no more a model for others to follow than was the Soviet Union. No country faces exactly the same conditions as another. But the once dominant paradigm that an expanding role in world trade is, for a developing country, a guaranteed formula for continued poverty and dependence on the West is hard to sustain against the overwhelming evidence to the contrary. Nowhere is the

5

resulting change in thinking more apparent than in China. It would be ironic if, just as the successful examples of open-economy growth were beginning to have a major impact toward more openness elsewhere in the developing world, the West, unable or unwilling to adjust to the resulting export expansion, were to turn its back on liberal economic policies and revert to protectionism.

Economic growth in East and Southeast Asia has also had a major influence on the politics of the region in both its domestic and international aspects. In the 1950s and 1960s security issues dominated most discussions of the future of Asia. The United States was in the midst of its third war in Asia, Soviet influence was expanding, and internal instability verging on civil war was rampant in the region. A major conflict between China and the Soviet Union by the late 1960s was no longer unthinkable.

Instability in the 1980s is largely confined to the Philippines, where two decades of government mismanagement have come home to roost, and to Indo-China, where aging Vietnamese leaders seem unable to shift away from a militarized society, still driven by goals only achievable through military means. Great power rivalry is muted in the region because most of the countries there are concentrating on their own affairs, notably on economic development. Development in turn has contributed to a long period of comparative stability in much of the region. Most important, China has become a force for stability, except vis-à-vis Vietnam, and perhaps, in a very different sense, Taiwan. China's increasing strength, built on rapid growth, makes a war with the Soviet Union less and less likely. The Chinese leadership's desire for a peaceful environment in which to build a strong and prosperous nation has led to efforts to reduce tensions on the Korean peninsula and elsewhere in Asia.

There is little doubt, therefore, that what happened first in Japan and then in the four smaller nations and territories of East Asia and now appears to have spread to China, is of enormous significance. It is important, that is, if the trends now underway continue. Is China really moving in the direction of the East Asian pattern of development? And, if it is, will it continue to do so for some decades ahead or will future leaders change course again? And, if future leaders do stay the course, will they achieve the kind of economic success realized by their East Asian predecessors or has the day of the "East Asian model" passed?

### THE EAST ASIAN PATTERN OF DEVELOPMENT

Before one can discuss whether China is or is not following in the footsteps of other East Asian developers and can speculate about the likelihood of their success in doing so, one must have a clearer picture of just what Japan and the other East Asian four achieved and how they did it. Only then can one return to the issue of the likely Chinese pattern of development in coming years and the features it will and will not have in common with its neighbors.

What then were the central characteristics of the economic development of Japan, Korea, Taiwan, Hong Kong, and Singapore?[2] Pointing out that all five were influenced by Confucian values, used Chinese characters, and ate with chopsticks, does not take one very far toward an understanding of economic growth in the region. The correlation between Confucian values and rapid economic development, for example, may be completely spurious. To demonstrate that the relationship is not spurious, one must show how those values acted positively on variables known to be important to development. Instead of starting with values and other indirect influences on economic growth, therefore, the discussion begins with an analysis of the direct causes of accelerated development and works back from there to more indirect relationships.

Economic growth is brought about either by an increase in inputs to production, primarily capital and labor, or by increases in the productivity of those inputs. In East Asia the capital stock did for a time grow even more rapidly than the high rates of increase in national product. In both Korea and Taiwan, for example, gross capital formation in the early stages of rapid growth was below 20 percent of gross domestic product (GDP), rising after a few years to 24 to 28 percent and then peaking before leveling off at above 30 percent of GDP. On the other hand, there was nothing remarkable about the rate of growth of the East Asian labor force. Population growth rates in Asia (except Japan) rose after World War II as death rates fell, and birth rates, for a time, fell more slowly. As these infants grew and entered the labor force in their late teens, the labor force growth rate rose to above 2 percent a year in much of the region.

If one places these capital and labor growth rates in a formal growth accounting framework, they account for about half of the 9 to 10 percent national product growth rates achieved for sustained periods in East Asia from the 1950s to the 1970s. The other half was accounted for by increases in productivity. The methodology underlying this conclusion is discussed in the appendix.

In searching for the underlying causes of high growth rates in East Asia, therefore, one must somehow explain this rapid increase in productivity. Showing that the Japanese saved an unusually high proportion of their personal income or that the Koreans and Japanese received large amounts of foreign aid (foreigners in part did the saving for them) explains only a portion of overall growth, and the smaller portion at that. As savings were converted into capital and new entrants to the labor force were hired, output increased much more rapidly than could be expected from the increase in these inputs alone. Most of Africa in the 1970s and early 1980s, for example, achieved substantial rates of capital formation and the labor force grew more rapidly than in East Asia, but national product growth rates in Africa in this period averaged only 3 percent a year. In Africa in the 1970s and early 1980s there was no increase in productivity and, in much of the region, a slight decline.

China prior to Mao Zedong's death in 1976 grew more rapidly than most of the nations of Africa, but the increase in Chinese gross national product can be accounted for almost entirely by the high rate of growth in the input of capital and labor. China's rate of capital formation, like that in Korea and Taiwan, rose from under 20 percent of gross domestic product in the 1950s to 30 percent and more in the early 1970s. But China's national product growth rate over the two decades 1955–57 to 1975–77 averaged only 5.1 percent a year, or less than 5 percent a year if the more realistic prices of the late 1970s are used to measure national product.[3] Since Mao's death, in contrast, China's rate of capital formation has fallen slightly and labor force growth has continued at 2 percent per annum, but the growth rate in national product in the nine years between 1977 and 1985 averaged over 8 percent a year. Productivity growth accounts for most of the change. If this growth rate could be sustained for another eighteen years, for twenty-seven altogether, Chinese GNP would reach eight times the level of 1976. In contrast, during the two and a half decades prior to 1976, GNP rose only about threefold. But is China entering into a period of sustained productivity growth as its neighbors did before it, or is China's current

9

performance unique to peculiarly Chinese conditions in the late 1970s and early 1980s and unlikely to be sustained?

## THE SOURCES OF PRODUCTIVITY GROWTH

The major difficulty in explaining productivity growth in East Asia is that economists do not know very much about what causes increases or declines in productivity growth in general. Some increases in productivity are imported from abroad in the form of new equipment that embodies advanced technology. Other important sources of productivity growth include improved management that makes it possible to use existing capital and labor resources more efficiently. A developing country also gains from being able to move labor out of low productivity occupations, notably peasant agriculture, into higher productivity urban industrial and service jobs. But why did East Asia do so much better than other nations in this area? Any answer to this question is bound to be speculative, but a review of East Asia's nineteenth- and twentieth-century experience provides some guidance.

To begin with, the nations of East Asia had a rich human resource base by pre-modern standards. A rich human resource base refers not to genetic traits that are probably randomly distributed across the globe, but to the way societies have been able to supplement the inherited talents of their populations through education and other kinds of experiences that have a direct bearing on economic development.

One clear difference between East Asia and many other parts of the developing world is the emphasis given to formal education. All nations in the region share a common Confucian heritage and Confucianism places great stress on education. In China and to a degree in Korea, this emphasis on education was reinforced by a system for selecting government officials that relied on formal examinations in the Confucian classics. The ability to read and write was also necessary for those involved in managing the quite sophisticated pre-modern commercial and banking systems of the region. This latter influence may have had much to do with Japan's high levels of literacy since government office was largely determined by heredity.

Whatever the precise reason, the result in Japan was a male population of whom half could read and write; in China the comparable figure was about one-third.[4] Literacy was much higher in urban than in rural areas and women received little formal education in either location. The percentage of Koreans who were literate in the use of their phonetic alphabet may have been very high, but those who could also read Chinese characters were probably fewer than in Japan.[5]

These figures on literacy do not seem impressive by the standards of the 1980s, but international comparisons are enlightening in this regard. Substantial parts of sub-Saharan Africa, for example, spoke languages for which there was no written version in the nineteenth century. As late as 1960 literacy in sub-Saharan Africa averaged only 16 percent of the adult population and in seven poor semi-arid nations the average was 3 percent. In that same year only 3 percent of the secondary school age-cohort actually attended a secondary school.[6]

Given the imprecision of estimates of literacy even today, systematic comparisons between East Asia and other parts of the world are not possible. One conclusion, however, is inescapable. It is impossible to build an education system overnight. A small oil-rich sultanate might be able to import all of its teachers from another better endowed Arabic-speaking nation, but most countries must train their own teachers and that takes time. One can staff schools with teachers who are only a little ahead of their students in terms of formal education, but the quality of education will suffer. Furthermore, much education takes place in the home, but the amount of education that takes place in homes where both parents are illiterate is limited, particularly with respect to skills relevant to a modern economy.

The nations of East Asia were in a position to staff a substantial and expanding formal education system from primary school through the university level by the early part of the twentieth century. Japan, of course, was well ahead of the others in this regard, but even China had a university enrollment of 40,000 in the early 1930s.[7] In all of sub-Saharan Africa in contrast, there were only about 70,000 students enrolled in secondary school as late as 1960. The number in 1930 was probably a few thousand at most. Those students were all that a region of over 200 million people had to staff its rapidly expanding education system and the emerging bureaucracies of forty about-to-be-independent countries, not to mention private sector requirements for education personnel. In short, Africa as late as 1960 was about where East Asia was in the nineteenth century.

But formal education is only part of the human resource story. Much education relevant to a modern economy is learned through experience. Experience with the management of large organizations is clearly useful. Knowledge of how markets work and how to manage credit is a part of any modern economic system. East Asia was well ahead of many other developing areas. Cities with a million or more people existed in East Asia long before the dawn of the twentieth century. To sustain cities of this size requires an elaborate commercial supply network to bring in food, fuel, and other necessities and luxuries. It took hundreds of thousands of people to operate these networks, and these people thus learned how to participate in and manage the process. Even the average peasant farmer was tied into this network and was exposed on a regular basis to the vicissitudes of market prices, the role of credit, and formal deeds and contracts. When the Europeans and Americans came to East Asia, they did not replace this system. Few foreigners were ever able to compete successfully in domestic East Asian markets and not many tried. The Europeans concentrated in foreign trade where their ships and superior knowledge of foreign markets gave them an advantage, but even this advantage was temporary. First Japanese and then Chinese businesses played an increasing role in foreign trade well before World War II. Only in colonial Hong Kong and Singapore did the rise to dominance of Chinese businessmen have to wait until the 1960s and 1970s.

Neither China nor Japan ever became a colony ruled by foreigners. Thus, Chinese and Japanese in large numbers also gained experience managing the organs of government. Korea, Taiwan, Hong Kong, and Singapore did not share in this experience, but they had compensating advantages at least as far as economic development is concerned. Millions of Koreans gained experience working in Japanese firms, not always at a low level, and living in an urban environment, often in Japan itself. Hong Kong and Singapore, of course, were primarily urban and residents there gained experience with urban life by definition. It is not entirely clear why urban life gives those who experience it a competitive advantage over those just off the farm, but there is ample evidence the world over to suggest that the advantage is real.

It is not necessary to go as far as Africa to find countries that missed out on this experience. Indonesia under the Dutch illustrates the main point. All government positions and most in large commercial organizations in what was then the Dutch East Indies were staffed, except at the most un-skilled levels, by Dutch. Small-scale commerce was largely the preserve of Chinese immigrants, brought in originally for other purposes, but who gravitated quickly to commerce where their experience from China and their organizational skills gave them a clear advantage over the local population. Since the Indonesians were mainly farmers, the Dutch saw little reason to educate them and some Dutch theorized that education, by bringing in modern values, would undermine Indonesian culture and hence do more harm than good. What education the people of Indonesia did receive was mainly connected with the reading of the Koran. The situation in much of Africa was even more extreme, with Europeans in a similar role and South Asians, Lebanese, and others taking the roles played by the Chinese in Southeast Asia.

East Asia's advantages in terms of education and experience were not unique in the developing world. Most developing nations would lie on a continuum in this regard, with East Asia at one end and much of sub-Saharan Africa at the other. As education systems around the world expand and as more experience with self-government is gained, the width from one end to the other of this continuum has narrowed, but it has not narrowed everywhere, and it has not been eliminated. The East Asian human resource base has in some respects pulled even further ahead by building vigorously on an already strong education base.

### POLITICS AND INSTABILITY

If East Asia as a whole possessed these human resource advantages, why did only Japan enter into sustained economic growth by the turn of the century, while the rest of East Asia did not get started until the 1950s or 1960s? Numerous ex-

planations have been put forward, many of which have focused on differences between Japan's more "feudal" social
structure and China's conservative bureaucratic state. While
some of these explanations have merit, they overlook the most
obvious explanation for why Japan started first and the others
didn't follow until five decades later.

It is extremely difficult to achieve sustained economic
growth if investors, public or private, must operate in an environment without security or predictability. It is often said
that political stability is necessary for growth, but the term
political stability is not very precise. Italian prime ministers
change every year or two but there is no comparable instability in the business environment. On the other hand, Mao Zedong ruled China uninterruptedly but the environment in
which investment decisions were made was fraught with un-
certainty between 1958 and 1976. The real issue, from the
point of view of economic development, therefore, is whether
a nation's political environment supports investors with a long
time-horizon.

By that standard Japan from the 1880s into the 1930s did
very well. Commodore Perry's "Black Ships" ended Japan's
isolation in 1854 and the Tokugawa Shogunate fell only fourteen years later. From 1868 until the 1930s Japan experienced
only one major political upheaval, the Satsuma Rebellion, and
that one was quickly suppressed. The next serious challenge
to the kind of government established in the Meiji period did
not come until the army officer corps began to take matters
into their own hands in a series of foreign adventures and
domestic assassinations that culminated in Japan's defeat in
1945. Before the army seized control, Japan experienced
nearly five decades of stable government. Equally important,
that government focused its attention on building a strong
economy and it had the resources to do so. Half of Japan's

capital formation was paid for out of government coffers and went to build the essential economic infrastructure. Japanese government officials saw support of private business as one of their principal duties. It is no accident that some of Japan's early great entrepreneurs, men such as Iwasaki of Mitsubishi and Shibusawa of the Dai Ichi Bank, had close ties to a government that could help them with contracts and other forms of support.

Japan's three decades of rapid growth following World War II have also been built on a base of a stable government oriented toward the promotion of economic development. For three decades Japan has been ruled by one political party and that party has been dominated by business interests. A stable international environment has been provided by Japan's alliance with the United States, which has made it possible for Japan to avoid diverting large resources away from investment into military expenditure.

The contrast with China's experience of the past century and a half is striking. China faced the Western imperialist challenge earlier than Japan, with defeat in the first Opium War in 1842, but the Qing emperors managed to cling to power for seven more decades. During those seven decades the dynasty experienced one major rebellion, that of the Taipings, and several lesser ones. The Taiping Rebellion lasted for fourteen years (1851–64), led to perhaps many millions of deaths, and destroyed large areas of the central and southern half of the country. While it was going on, China lost a second war with the Western powers (1857–60), which further reduced the nation's control over its own port cities.

With the end of the Taiping Rebellion, China did enjoy three decades of comparative peace but the government was split between a few viceroys in the provinces who tried to begin the modernization process and the court in Beijing which saw little need for fundamental change. Furthermore, the Qing imperial government had few financial resources under its control with which to promote economic development even if it had wished to do so. Chinese government revenues in the nineteenth century were never more than 2 percent of China's gross national product, as contrasted to several times that level in Japan, and those revenues were largely committed to routine government administration and the military.[8]

In retrospect, the three decades between 1865 and 1894 were China's last chance for development before 1949. In 1895 China was defeated in war by Japan and lost Taiwan. Reform attempts in 1898 failed, and the conservative reaction that caused the failure combined with the Boxer Rebellion to bring about another Western invasion and defeat in 1901. The dynasty collapsed in 1911 and Yuan Shih-kai's attempts to found a new dynasty ended in 1918. For the next decade China was controlled by regional warlords jockeying for power. The Kuomintang was able to establish a semblance of unity in 1928, but the Communists had broken away and had begun the rebellion that was to lead them to victory in 1949. In 1931 Japan seized China's northeastern provinces and in 1937 invaded China proper in a war that did not end until 1945, eight years later. Instead of peace, however, China between 1945 and 1949 experienced all-out civil war.

Given this history there is not much of a mystery to why China failed to enter into a sustained period of economic growth before 1949. Investors, to the extent they could find security at all, found it in the treaty ports controlled by the imperial powers or in Japanese-controlled Manchuria. Industrial development did take place there, but in too limited a fashion to bring about a fundamental restructuring of the Chinese economy. Only in 1949 did China achieve unity and stability under a government committed to promoting economic development and able to mobilize the resources necessary for the task. Even after 1949 the commitment of the Chinese government to modern economic growth was incomplete and the limited nature of that commitment has much to do with the nation's slow productivity growth through 1976.

The other four nations or territories with which these essays are concerned enjoyed political stability throughout the first part of the twentieth century until 1941. All four did in fact experience a substantial rise in per capita gross national product in this period to the degree that limited data and limited previous research allow us to tell. But much of the growth was of the peculiarly colonial variety. The extreme case is Korea where a sustained rise in per capita GNP over three decades was accompanied by a fall in the standard of living of most Koreans.[9] Japanese businesses and Japanese and Korean landlords reaped most of the benefits. Taiwan did much better with a per capita GNP of nearly four hundred dollars (in 1981 prices) in the 1930s and with the people of Taiwan the main beneficiaries,[10] but Taiwan's economy was still largely agricultural. Hong Kong and Singapore's prosperity was built on commerce with very little industry, and the dominant commercial firms were mostly British. Thus each of these four areas made some economic gains during the pre-war colonial period, but a key ingredient of modern economic growth was missing. The people of these countries or territories participated in the growth as workers or farmers and sometimes as beneficiaries of rising per capita incomes, but not as entrepreneurs or managers or engineers of the more modern enterprises.

After Japan's defeat in 1945, stability was restored quickly to Hong Kong and growth resumed, but no longer with just British firms in the lead. Shanghai businessmen fleeing the

Communists set up their factories in the New Territories and began the Chinese dominated industrialization process that gave the colony a per capita GNP of over five thousand dollars by the early 1980s.

At the opposite extreme was South Korea that went through five years of instability after Japan's surrender, followed by three years of war that left the physical infrastructure of the nation in rubble. There was political stability of a sort for the seven years that followed the war, until student demonstrations brought down the government of Syngman Rhee, but President Rhee while in office had little interest in economic affairs and pursued political goals and policies that made development, even with massive American aid, extremely difficult. The coup that brought Park Chung Hee to power ushered in seventeen years of consistent and uninterrupted government support for economic development.

Singapore's experience was much like Hong Kong's except that political stability was less complete during the years leading up to Singapore's independence in 1959 and brief interlude of being part of Malaysia in the early 1960s, and Singapore's political stability since then has been the result of indigenous forces, not a colonial administration. The results, however, have been much like those of Hong Kong, with per capita GNP passing five thousand dollars by the early 1980s. Taiwan did not face the kind of political turmoil experienced by Korea in the 1950s, but the Kuomintang government did have to settle two million refugees from the mainland and organize to ward off a possible attack by Communist forces. Despite these difficulties, GNP growth averaged 7 percent a year from 1952 through 1960.

As this brief review of East Asian history makes clear, periods of rapid economic growth in the region coincided with governments that were stable for long periods of time and which gave a high priority to creating a climate conducive to investment in growth. Periods of stagnation or decline in the economy most often coincided with wars and civil wars or their immediate aftermath. Pre-World War II colonial governments fit this pattern as well except that the leaders and largest beneficiaries of economic growth were foreigners rather than local people.

It does not follow that all nations need to do to achieve economic development is to introduce stable political regimes dedicated to economic growth. In East Asia, however, political stability under an independent sovereign government was the missing ingredient. Once such a government was in place, the region's rich human resource base came into play and rapid growth followed.

## EAST ASIAN ECONOMIC SYSTEMS

The above view appears to some degree to be in conflict with one that attributes East Asia's growth experience to the economic system and the economic policies pursued by these nations. Economists such as Milton Friedman have gone so far as to attribute the rapid growth of part of East Asia in the 1960s and 1970s to the adoption of laissez-faire capitalism. Hong Kong does in fact seem to fit the view that the government that governs best in economic affairs is the one that governs least. Singapore was also a completely open economy from the start, although the government has played an activist role in setting wages and promoting certain sectors.

The real difficulty with the laissez-faire image is when it is used to describe South Korea, Taiwan, or Japan. The history of Korean shipbuilding illustrates the point. In the early 1970s President Park called in the head of the Hyundai conglomerate and asked him to explore establishing a major shipbuilding enterprise in Korea. After a period of exploring what the establishment of such an enterprise would entail, the head of Hyundai returned to say that the task was too difficult. Korea had little relevant experience to build upon and it would be best to wait until more such experience had been gained. President Park, it is reported, stated that Hyundai's conclusion was understandable, but if Hyundai only wanted to do the easy tasks, it needn't bother to turn to the government for help in the future. Since much of Hyundai's business had been built up in cooperation with the government, this threat to withdraw support led Hyundai to reverse its decision to go into shipbuilding. Not much over a year later the first Korean supertanker was launched, but it was launched into a market saturated with supertankers. President Park's government, however, came to the rescue with a rule giving advantages to those who imported petroleum into Korea in Korean-made tankers. A few years later Korea had become one of the leading shipbuilders in the world.[11]

However one describes this system of government-business cooperation, it is not laissez faire. It is an economic system where the government plays an active role, not only in providing infrastructure, but in giving guidance backed by concrete rewards and penalties to the private sector as well. In addition to promoting exports, government in Korea actively pushed import substitution through the use of high tariffs and other restrictions on imports. Anyone who has studied the economic systems of Japan and Taiwan would see obvious parallels with Korea. Iwasaki, the founder of Mitsubishi, was helped along in the nineteenth century by government purchases of his woolens for uniforms and government use of his ships as military transports. In more recent times, the role of the Ministry of International Trade and Industry (MITI) in Japan has been the focus of numerous studies of how government can guide industry.

Government planning of this sort has not always been right or successful. MITI's attempt to consolidate the Japanese automobile industry was ignored or circumvented by the companies involved, with results that can be seen in parking lots and show windows all over the United States. The Korean government's emphasis on heavy industries in the 1970s is seen as one possible source of economic difficulties in the late 1970s and early 1980s, although many of these heavy industries have gone on to become major exporters. But for all the mistakes, the system clearly did not undermine productivity growth in any fundamental way. Similar import substitution policies and government direction elsewhere in the world, in contrast, have helped create inefficient enterprises unable to compete in the outside world.

In the results it has achieved, why is East Asia so different from much of Latin America? The answer presumably lies in the fact that Latin American owners and managers of import substituting enterprises could obtain sufficient political support to maintain high levels of protection and avoid the need to become more efficient. East Asian entrepreneurs, for some reason too complex to explore here, could not or did not form the necessary political alliances. Protection was given on a temporary basis to allow them a chance to learn by doing and then was gradually reduced or eliminated.

Does it follow that, given political stability, East Asia's rich human resource base can make any economic system work efficiently? The test cases for this proposition are the centrally planned, fully socialist, and autarkic systems of North Korea and Mao Zedong's China. Both did achieve sustained increases in per capita income over long periods of time with this system, but neither was able to attain high rates of growth in productivity.[12] Because growth was brought about almost entirely by increased inputs alone, the rates realized, as indicated earlier, were well below those of the truly rapid developers of East Asia.

Part of any attempt to forecast whether China can achieve the high economic performance of a Japan or a South Korea, therefore, involves making a judgment about China's ability to modify its economic system sufficiently to achieve high rates of growth in productivity. Clearly that does not require China to go all the way to laissez-faire capitalism, nor does it necessarily mean attempting to copy Japan's system. The key is to create a planning system that at least does not block the kinds of innovations needed for rapid increases in productivity. Whether or not China will be able to create such a system is a major theme of the second essay.

ECONOMIC POLICIES

Most development economists attempting to explain East Asian growth would pass quickly over the above issues if they did not ignore them altogether. Economists are used to taking the economic and political systems and the human resource base as a given parameter, not as a variable. They focus instead on the specific policies pursued by governments.

Most economists would agree that the outward oriented policies of Japan and the East Asian four were an important ingredient in their success. Outward orientation is probably directly related to high productivity growth, although the argument cannot be proved in any very scientific way. The gains are not so much those associated with static comparative advantage, although those gains are part of the story. Of equal or greater significance are the effects on productivity of the need to be able to compete in foreign markets. Also important is the ability of an exporting nation to import more advanced technology and overcome temporary shortages of key intermediate inputs because exports have provided it with ample reserves of foreign exchange.

Once one moves beyond the outward orientation of these East Asian nations' economic strategies, it is difficult to find other specific economic policies that were central to their economic success. Books have been written about Korea's interest rate reforms and how they raised savings and increased the efficiency of Korean capital markets by eliminating "financial repression."[13] More recent works, however, have called into question the importance of these reforms, not least because the Korean government did not long stay with the high real interest rates that were a central feature of those reforms.

Another popularly held view is that foreign direct investment had much to do with East Asia's economic performance. Far from being a hindrance to economic development as the literature on dependency would have it, multinationals played a leading role in East Asia. Some support for this view can be found in the cases of Hong Kong and Singapore, although the most dynamic elements in both economies are local Chinese and Chinese elsewhere in Southeast Asia with ties to Hong Kong and Singapore firms. But it is difficult to see how the argument has much validity in the case of Japan, South Korea, or Taiwan. Japan, in particular, was consistently hostile to any influx of foreign direct investment until virtually forced to open its capital markets under threat of retaliation on Japanese exports. Foreign direct investment in Korea averaged under $10 million a year (in U.S. dollars) in the 1960s and about $100 million in the 1970s. Taiwan's annual average was a bit higher at about $40 million in the 1960s and $180 million in the 1970s, but these averages are based on approvals, not foreign investment actually realized. Even the figures based on approvals represent less than 5 percent of total gross capital formation in South Korea and Taiwan during these two decades.[14] The overwhelming share in the ownership and control of Korean and Taiwan enterprises was in the hands of local people, not foreigners.

While South Korea and Taiwan erected subtle barriers to foreign ownership and control, they welcomed the inflow of foreign capital in other forms. Korea has borrowed heavily from both commercial banks and the international lending agencies. Korea's debt of over $40 billion makes it one of the largest borrowers in the developing world, but Korea's strong export performance also means that this debt has not generated difficult repayment problems. Taiwan in contrast has borrowed very little in recent years from either commercial banks or the international lending agencies and, with large balance of payments surpluses in the 1980s, is a net creditor.

Both Korea and Taiwan in the 1950s and 1960s were major recipients of U.S. grant aid and some analysts have suggested that this massive aid has had much to do with their economic success. U.S. aid to Taiwan did average over $100 million a year in the 1950s, a figure close to the island's total capital formation during that decade. But U.S. economic assistance came to an end after 1965 just as the GNP growth rate was accelerating. Thus aid played a crucial role in making it possible for the mainlanders to resettle two million of their number on the island and to introduce various reforms and establish political control while incomes rose. But the high rates of productivity growth of the latter half of the 1960s and the 1970s occurred without significant inflow of aid.

Economic grant aid to Korea was substantially larger than that to Taiwan and lasted longer. Aid receipts from the end of the Korean War through 1960 averaged U.S. $270 million a year, falling to an average of $140 million a year in the next decade. The last year of significant economic aid inflow was 1971, although economic assistance was not formally ended until the mid-1970s. To what extent does this aid inflow account for Korea's high rate of growth? Certainly it is difficult to imagine Korea's achieving rapid recovery from massive wartime destruction without U.S. assistance. In the 1960s as well, imports would have had to have been sharply curtailed in the absence of aid, given that Korea began the decade with hardly any export earnings at all. Aid also made it easier to introduce certain economic reforms, but the influence of aid on policy was mixed at best. It is doubtful, for example, whether the Rhee government could have continued its disastrous anti-growth economic policies (prohibition on trade with Japan, a badly overvalued exchange rate) if it had not been able to count on the flow of U.S. assistance. Ironically, President Kennedy's threats to reduce aid after the military coup of 1961 may have encouraged some of the more significant economic reforms. The threat was made to induce a return to Korea's brief experiment with democratic politics, but the conclusion probably drawn by the generals was that they had better find an alternative to U.S. aid if they wanted to reduce U.S. influence on Korean domestic affairs.[15] The only option effectively open to them, as they discovered over the next several years, was to promote the export of manufactures.

The final area of policy reform that warrants mention in this brief discussion of the sources of East Asian growth is land reform. Japan, South Korea, and Taiwan all experienced a major transfer of land from landlords to peasant tillers in the late 1940s and early 1950s. Furthermore, the transfer of land titles, particularly in Korea and Japan, involved a substantial element of confiscation without compensation to the landlords. There was, as a result, significant redistribution of wealth to former tenant farmers. At the same time war had destroyed the urban assets of most people in Korea and Japan and the withdrawal of Japanese colonials provided another source of redistributed wealth in Korea and Taiwan. As a result of these measures, therefore, these three countries or regions began the post-war era with an unusual degree of income equality.

Economists know relatively little about how income inequality affects growth. The common assumption of many growth models that inequality is necessary in order to promote savings is almost certainly false. If this assumption were true in most cases, it would be difficult to explain how East Asia had achieved such high rates of savings and capital formation starting from a base with such low levels of inequality.

It may be that the main gain for economic development from reduced inequality works indirectly through politics rather than directly on economic behavior. East Asia in the 1950s came closer to providing equal opportunity for economic success than most developing societies. Everyone, to some degree therefore, had a stake in policies that made rapid development possible, although not all realized this or took advantage of the opportunity. Still, many did and others benefited from their initiative. The benefits of growth in East Asia were widely distributed. And this wide distribution in turn contributed to political stability that made further growth possible. Certainly there was nothing inherently popular about the military government of Korea or the mainlander-dominated government of Taiwan except for the economic successes and stability that they achieved. Nor would the Liberal-Democratic party of Japan have enjoyed such a long reign if the nation had been wracked by periodic depressions followed by slow growth, or if all the benefits had gone to the executives of the large conglomerates.

Again Latin America provides an obvious basis for comparison. In Brazil and Mexico, the top 20 percent of the people receive over 60 percent of the national income, over twelve times the per capita share of the bottom 40 percent of the people. In Japan, Korea, and Taiwan the top 20 percent receive 40 percent (45 percent in Korea) or only four times the per capita share of the bottom 40 percent of the people.[16] A sense of equality of opportunity in much of Latin America is made all the more difficult by deep ethnic cleavages between those of Spanish descent and those whose ancestors were native to the continent.

It would take this essay too far afield to compare the politics of urban elites in Latin America with the politics of East Asia where rural populations play a larger role except in the city states. Such a comparison, however, would likely conclude that reduced inequality and a widely shared sense of economic opportunity contributed to greater political stability in the one region whereas the lack of such conditions contributed to instability and policies inimical to growth in the other.

What is the relevance of this discussion of the sources of growth in Japan, South Korea, Taiwan, Singapore, and Hong Kong to an understanding of China's present and future economic performance? The argument has been that rapid growth in these East Asian nations and territories can be explained first by a rich human resource base and sustained periods of stable growth-oriented governments. A wide range of economic systems and policies appear to have been consistent with high productivity growth, but a few elements appear to exist in all or most of the rapid developers. All pursued an open economy policy that stressed the export of manufactures. Most started from a base of sharply reduced income inequality and few class or ethnic barriers to opportunity. None of the rapid developers practiced centrally planned socialism, but three of them did allow for an active government role in investment and in providing guidance to the private sector.

China in the 1980s starts from a human resource base as strong as that of the 1950s in Korea and Taiwan. Income inequality was reduced sharply by land reform in the 1940s and early 1950s, and urban inequality declined as most wealthy individuals either fled the country or lost most of their assets. Since 1977 the country has followed an open economic policy with an emphasis on the export of manufactures. Political leadership has been stable since 1979 and economic policy overall has been characterized by a spirit of pragmatic experimentation designed to achieve rapid growth. The main difference between China and its East Asian neighbors is its size and the fact that industry is still largely run according to the rules of Soviet-style central planning. The main questions about the future have to do with whether China will move away from central planning toward more indirect forms of guidance of a still socialist industry, and whether the political leadership will continue to provide support for such a move. These latter issues are the subject of chapter 2. Here the main point is that China shares many important characteristics with its neighbors in East Asia. If it can come up with an urban economic system that operates efficiently, and if the international system accommodates expanding Chinese exports, there is every reason to believe that China can achieve growth rates approaching those elsewhere in East Asia. The caveats are important ones, but the likelihood of Chinese economic success is high enough to make it worthwhile to explore some of the implications of rapid economic growth.

In terms of per capita gross national product, China in the mid-1980s is about where South Korea and Taiwan were in the 1950s. To make these comparisons one must convert per capita GNP into U.S. dollars at some given year's prices. There are both theoretical and practical problems with such conversions and the estimates as a result are imprecise. Roughly, Taiwan's 1952 per capita GNP in 1981 prices was about U.S. $400 and that of South Korea in 1963 was about $500 in comparable prices. In the early 1980s, converted at the official exchange rate of 1982 or 1983, Chinese GNP per capita would be about $300, but the Chinese official exchange rate probably understates Chinese GNP relative to what it would be if calculated more systematically.[17] Whether the correct figure is $350 or $450 matters little for this analysis.

As economic development proceeds, there are two changes in structure that invariably occur. In every nation that has undergone sustained growth to date, there has been a steady decline in the share of national product originating from the agricultural sector and a rise in the share of industry. Second, the rising share of industry has been accompanied by a major shift in population out of rural and into urban areas.

Each country's pattern differs somewhat from that of another, but, in general, the faster the rate of growth of per capita GNP, the more rapid is the structural transformation out of agriculture and the rural areas into industry and urbanization. The East Asian experience in this regard is illustrated in Tables 1 and 2. Singapore and Hong Kong are ex-

TABLE 1

## Industrial Shares in National Product

| Republic of Korea | 1962 | 1970 | 1975 | 1980 |
|---|---|---|---|---|
| Per capita GNP (US 1980 $) | 475 | 810 | 1,140 | 1,490 |
| Agriculture share in GNP (%) | 43.3 | 30.4 | 24.9 | 15.9 |
| Industry share in GNP (%) | 16.0 | 30.8 | 40.6 | 52.4 |
| Taiwan | 1952 | 1960 | 1970 | 1980 |
| Per capita N.I. (US 1980 $) | 430 | 570 | 1,120 | 2,100 |
| Agriculture share in NDP (%) | 35.9 | 32.8 | 17.9 | 9.3 |
| Industry share in NDP | 21.9 | 29.0 | 40.6 | 51.6 |
| Japan | 1910 | 1930 | 1953 | 1965 |
| Per capita GNP (US 1980 $) | 1,100 | 1,600 | 1,400 | 4,000 |
| Agriculture share in NDP (%) | 26.8 | 19.8 | 17.5 | 7.7 |
| Industry share in NDP (%) | 22.5 | 40.3 | 42.5 | 54.0 |

*Sources methodology:* The agriculture and industry share figures are taken from Economic Planning Board, *Major Statistics of the Korean Economy, 1982* (Seoul: EPB, 1982). The share figures for Korea are in constant 1975 prices. The Taiwan share data are from Council for Economic Planning and Development, *Taiwan Statistical Data Book, 1983* (Taipei, 1983), p. 25. The Japanese figures are from Kazushi Ohkawa and Henry Rosovsky, *Japanese Economic Growth* (Stanford: Stanford University Press, 1973), pp. 284–85. The Taiwan agriculture and industry data are in current prices and those for Japan in constant prices. Industry here includes all sectors other than services and agriculture, fisheries and forestry.

The per capita income figures, unlike the industry and agricultural share data, are in constant 1980 U.S. dollars and were derived starting with World Bank estimates of GNP per capita and working backwards using real growth rates in per capita income estimated in the above sources. The Taiwan figures are from the above source for other Taiwan data and are for national income per capita rather than GNP per capita.

TABLE 2
Agriculture's Share in Total Employment

| Republic of Korea | | Taiwan | | Japan | |
|---|---|---|---|---|---|
| Year | Share % | Year | Share % | Year | Share % |
| 1963 | 63.1 | 1952 | 56.1 | 1910 | 62.5 |
| 1970 | 50.4 | 1960 | 50.2 | 1930 | 49.6 |
| 1975 | 45.5 | 1970 | 36.7 | 1953 | 42.4 |
| 1980 | 34.0 | 1980 | 19.5 | 1965 | 25.5 |

*Sources:* The figures are from the same sources used to derive Table 1.

cluded since neither had much of a rural or agricultural sector to start with. Their rural hinterlands lay on the other side of international boundaries. At the beginning of their periods of rapid sustained economic growth, the share of agriculture in the national product of Taiwan and South Korea was two to three times that of industry. Thirty years later in Taiwan the share of industry was five times that of agriculture and twenty years later in Korea the industry ratio was two and a half times that of agriculture. Agricultural nations in a single generation had been transformed into industrial nations. Japan's transformation, of course, occurred earlier and took longer because Japanese growth rates in the pre-World War II era, when part of this transition occurred, were much slower than in the post-war period. The data on employment in Table 2 tell a similar story.

Will China's population go through a similar transition away from agriculture and rural residence and into urban areas and urban occupations? Industry's share in GNP already matched that of agriculture by the 1970s, but employment is still heavily concentrated in farming where 70 percent of those employed in 1983 worked. Thus by one measure, China's economic structure is comparable to that of Taiwan and Korea when those areas had per capita incomes of $600 to $800 in 1980 U.S. prices. By the other measure, however, China has employment shares comparable to some of the poorer nations in the world, nations with per capita incomes not much above $200. The reasons for this inconsistency with international averages and whether China's pattern is about to change, perhaps quickly and dramatically, are the subject of chapter 2.

Some additional consequences of the East Asian growth experience are worthy of note and raise questions about what might happen to China over the next two decades. One consequence that is visible even to the casual visitor to East Asia is the transition to a consumer durable society. Increasing proportions of family incomes are spent on television sets and refrigerators, items that have appeal the world over. As refrigerators become the norm, it is no longer necessary to buy vegetables fresh every day. The impact of television is more profound. It was a rare farmhouse or urban apartment in Taiwan or South Korea in the early 1980s that did not sprout a TV aerial. Images of other ways of life from around the world can be beamed into the family livingroom. The potential impact on a society's values is enormous and governments frequently try to limit or control that impact. The Korean government in 1985, for example, asked the United States to restrict the beaming of the Armed Forces Korea Network (AFKN) to U.S. bases and to shorten hours because Korean youth were made "defenseless before the advanced country's culture and dependent upon that culture."[18] The AFKN situation is unusual, but, even when government censorship is universal, government control over what people learn from what they see on television is far from complete.

The automobile also can change fundamentally how people live, and Korea, Taiwan, and the two city states have entered the automobile stage of consumption. Korea in the early 1980s had only 500,000 private automobiles, but that is more per capita than in Japan in the early 1960s. Taiwan, with half of Korea's population, had over 600,000 private motor vehicles. Automobiles require roads to run on, service stations to sell gasoline, and roadside restaurants where travelers can eat. And autos are really only a part of a broader transport revolution that has made the entire population of Japan and the East Asian four highly mobile. It is doubtful that there is anyone in these countries or territories who has not visited and stayed for a while in a major city. Few Koreans live more than an hour by inexpensive bus from a major city and most do not live more than four hours from Seoul. A few decades ago in East Asia one could still speak of a large peasant population that lived and died in its native villages with only rare glimpses if any of the world beyond the market town. Now the majority of the people live in major cities, and the rest have relatives there whom they can visit easily.

Rapid economic growth has been largely responsible for marked changes in people's health in East Asia. In Taiwan over the past quarter century the life expectancy of the population rose by ten years to seventy years for males and seventy-five years for females (in 1982). Life-threatening communicable diseases are no more a problem in much of East Asia than they are in Western Europe or North America.

Other social changes have also been profound. All of these areas of East Asia have largely completed the demographic transition which begins with a fall in death rates and accelerated population growth and ends when birth rates fall far enough to bring down the population growth rate. By the early 1980s the population growth rate had fallen to 1.9 percent per year in Taiwan and 1.6 percent a year in Korea. The total fertility rate of all women in Taiwan had fallen from over 6 in the 1950s to under 2.5 in the early 1980s. Accompanying the decline in total fertility and perhaps helping cause it were changes in the status and role of women. In 1953 in Taiwan there were under two thousand women students enrolled in universities in Taiwan, 15 percent of the total, although women already accounted for 28 percent of secondary school enrollments. By 1982 the share of women in secondary and tertiary education was 48 and 42 percent, respectively.

Economic development in East Asia, it is clear, made possible a fundamental transformation of East Asian society. In Japan the process began around the beginning of the twentieth century. In the other four rapid developers there was some progress before World War II but most of the change occurred in the 1960s and 1970s. By the early 1980s the way of life of the majority of the people in this region would have been more familiar to urban residents in Europe or North America than it would have been to the East Asian people's own ancestors. There were a few Koreans and Chinese who were very rich and a much larger number who were poor and existed on the margin of society, but the dominant culture was that of the urban "middle class." In Japan 90 percent of the population identified itself as middle class. The numbers in Korea, Taiwan, Hong Kong, and Singapore would not be so high but the trend was in that direction.

Given this social transformation that has accompanied economic development, the lack of comparable changes in the political sphere is a bit surprising. Japan, to be sure, has a genuinely democratic system where votes are as honestly counted as anywhere else and the opposition is free to criticize with as much vigor as it chooses. But even in Japan rule is by one party, and four decades after Japan's surrender in 1945 there was still no opposition party with a credible chance of forming a government. The European and American form of democracy, where a loyal opposition periodically replaces the governing party, simply does not exist in East Asia.

Among the other four East Asian states, Singapore has elections but opposition organizing and compaigning is rigorously curtailed. The Republic of Korea also has elections and an active political opposition but, with one exception that lasted only one year, governments have been formed by military coup d'etat and other non-democratic means since Korea regained its independence from Japan. In Taiwan opposition figures get elected to local office, but the Kuomintang party still controls all of the major levers of power and presidents have held office for life. Hong Kong has a governor general appointed by the British government and no elections of consequence.

As pointed out earlier, these governments over the past several decades have provided a stable environment for investment and rapid growth. But are these political foundations for development likely to persist into the future? Is the one-party state that holds office for decades at a time a normal reflection of East Asian culture, including particularly the Confucian tradition of hierarchy and respect for authority? Or are the East Asian governments of the 1950s through the 1980s a product of an era of transition from an imperial-colonial and peasant-based traditional polity to some new and as yet untried form, democratic or otherwise? And, if this transition occurs, will it be smooth or will it be accompanied by long periods of political turmoil and economic stagnation?

The reason for reintroducing the role of politics at this point in the discussion is to emphasize that East Asia's transformation to a modern society is not yet complete except in Japan, and politics will have much to say about how and even

whether the modernization process will continue. If this statement is true about the states on China's East Asian periphery,
how much more true is it of China itself? In the essay that
follows, the main theme is that China in the mid-1980s is in
the early stages of the same development process that has so
radically transformed first Japan and more recently Korea,
Taiwan, Hong Kong, and Singapore. Whether China will in
fact see that process through to a complete transformation to
a modern urban and industrial society depends as much on
politics as it does on the accumulation of capital and advanced
technology.

# 2

## *Is China Following the East Asian Pattern?*

Economic growth in a number of countries and territories in East Asia had characteristics of its own that distinguished it sharply from the experiences of Latin America or Africa and even from the growth patterns of South Asia. China, however, from the beginning of the People's Republic in 1949 until the death of Mao Zedong in 1976 followed a different path from its East Asian neighbors.

Like its East Asian neighbors, China in 1949 had a Confucian heritage that emphasized education and provided the nation with many people who were literate and with a small but significant highly educated elite. Pre-modern urban and commercial development brought relevant experience to tens of millions of Chinese citizens. To this relatively rich foundation of human resources, the Chinese Communist party added the ingredients that had been missing under previous regimes.

For the first time since the 1870s and 1880s the Communists achieved both unity and an end to internal strife. But unlike the Imperial government of the late nineteenth century, the government of the People's Republic set out to mobilize the resources necessary for development. Taxes, which accounted for only 2 percent of gross national product in the nineteenth century, were raised after 1949 to a point well above 30 percent of GNP. And the largest share of these taxes was channeled into capital formation. Education was also expanded rapidly in order to strengthen the human resource base and facilitate the import of modern technology, mainly from the Soviet Union and Eastern Europe. The expanded university population was directed away from the humanities and social sciences into engineering and the natural sciences. Many thousands of Chinese were sent for post-graduate training in these subjects to the Soviet Union and ten thousand Soviet advisors came to China to help with the industrialization effort. Inequality due to wide disparities in the ownership of property was eliminated by a thoroughgoing land reform and by the state takeover of most urban property.

In these respects China's experience in the 1950s was much like that of its East Asian neighbors with the one distinction that China's technical and financial assistance came from the Soviet Union rather than the United States. China was also poorer than either Taiwan or South Korea in the 1950s, mainly because China in the period from 1910 to 1949 was engulfed in war and civil war while South Korea and Taiwan experienced stability and some growth under colonial regimes.

The most important distinctions between China and its neighbors, however, were not those connected with differences in per capita GNP. China, as pointed out in chapter 1, introduced an economic system and a development strategy that had little in common with those of Japan or the rest of East Asia. China's choices were in important respects carbon copies of those made in the 1930s by the Soviet Union. Like the Soviet Union then, China in the 1950s saw itself surrounded by hostile forces, which made an emphasis on machinery and steel rather than consumer goods both a means to more rapid growth and a way to strengthen the nation's defensive capacity. China in the 1950s did import large quantities of investment goods, but this was seen as an unfortunate necessity. Dependence on imported goods was to be reduced as rapidly as was feasible. The goal was autarky even if it was a long way from being achieved. Exports, mainly agricultural products and a few minerals, were necessary in order to pay for essential imports, but served no other purpose.

Along with this closed economy, heavy industry strategy went the decision carried out in 1955 and 1956 to fully socialize the economy. All but the smallest petty traders and industrial producers were taken over by the state. Agriculture was fully collectivized with agricultural producer cooperatives in 1956 and then with the formation of People's Communes in 1958. In agriculture, market forces were allowed to continue to play a role in the allocation of consumer goods and in the sale of minor farm products, but in industry the market was replaced by central planning and administrative allocation of key inputs on the Soviet pattern.

Partly because of and partly in spite of these changes, China's economic growth rate accelerated from the negligible levels of the 1930s and 1940s to 7 or 8 percent per year in the first five-year plan period (1953–57). Despite this early economic success, however, elements in the Chinese leadership, notably Mao Zedong, were not satisfied. Mao's messianic vision for China was driven by values many of which had little to do with economics, but in 1958 and 1959, at least, that vision included the belief that China could find a new and faster way to achieve economic development and the creation of a Communist society. That vision was inspired by neither the Soviet Union nor the rest of East Asia, but by Mao's own experience with attaining seemingly unreachable goals through mobilization of the masses. Growth in the rest of East Asia would not have inspired anyone in 1958 when Mao launched the Great Leap Forward. Japan's economic boom was only a few years old and that of the others in East Asia had not yet started. Few Japanese anticipated that their boom would continue uninterrupted for two decades.

The collapse of the Great Leap Forward in 1960 ended the extreme forms of the mass mobilization approach to economic development. China's economic policy for the next sixteen years settled into an uneasy tug-of-war between those who wanted to return to a Soviet-style emphasis on central planning and heavy industry and those who still saw economic virtues in mass mobilization, albeit on a more limited scale and confined largely to rural areas. Those on the mass mobilization side of the scale were also interested in reducing the role of material incentives in motivating worker and peasant effort. Wage differentials were retained as were differences in incomes between rural regions and communes, but most of the incentive features of these differentials were removed. Throughout the 1960s and early 1970s almost no one was promoted from one wage grade to another, regardless of performance. Work points in the rural areas were awarded with only limited attention to the work effort of the recipient and were changed infrequently.

There was also an ongoing debate over the proper role of foreign trade and imported technology, but neither side of the debate evinced any interest in what has come to be called export-led growth. Those associated with Mao criticized almost all aspects of foreign technology and suggested that China's people, even uneducated peasants, could do better. Those on the other side of the argument simply stated that it didn't make sense to waste resources reinventing the wheel. In certain sectors, notably petrochemicals, it was more efficient to import plants from abroad.

The arguments over material incentives and the role of foreign technology waxed and waned. Depending in part on the

44

relative strength of the opposing forces, imports of plant and equipment rose or fell. But outside the trade sphere and to a degree even within it there was a surprising consistency to China's economic policy. The rhetoric was to take agriculture as the foundation, but throughout the 1962–76 period most investment went to heavy industry and related infrastructure. There were vigorous attacks on the bureaucracy and during the early phase of the Cultural Revolution (1966–69), the central ministries in Beijing were stripped of personnel, as was the planning commission. But central planning and the administrative allocation of most industrial inputs were retained. The one change was the decentralization of much planning to the provinces and, in the case of small-scale industry, even to the county level. In the countryside there were experiments with brigade-level management (a unit of several hundred families), but most agricultural production remained under the control of the production team, a smaller unit of twenty to thirty families. Private plots representing about 7 percent of the cultivated area were criticized, as were rural markets on which the products of those plots were sold, but both continued to exist even if in a somewhat restricted form.

The results of these policies and debates for China's economy were far from disastrous. Only at the height of the political activity of the Cultural Revolution, in 1967 and 1968, was there a decline in industrial production and perhaps in GNP. Agriculture suffered even less, falling only in 1972 and then mainly because of poor weather. Even if one includes the period of the Great Leap Forward and its aftermath, the average rate of growth of GNP between 1957 and 1976 was between 4 and 5 percent a year depending on whether early or late year Chinese prices are used to value output.[1]

But the economy was becoming increasingly inefficient. Energy in particular was being used profligately. By one estimate China was using two and a half times as much energy per dollar of national product as India,[2] and India is itself considered to be inefficient in its use of resources. Only the discovery of the Daqing oil field and the rapid development of China's petroleum industry made it possible for GNP growth to continue at a fairly high level despite the waste of energy.

Per capita GNP was growing at about 2½ percent a year but consumer incomes and consumption were not growing this fast. The share of GNP going to capital formation rose steadily and there may also have been some increase in the proportion of output going to the military. Increases in two- and three-worker families in the cities meant family income was rising despite the freeze on wages. Rural incomes grew more slowly because agricultural production just kept up with population growth at 2 percent a year. What increase in rural incomes occurred did so because of rises in the prices paid by the state for grain and other crops.

Could this economic system with this level of performance have continued indefinitely into the future? There is no obvious crisis that would have brought the economy to a halt and forced change. The rapid growth in petroleum output in the mid-1970s was about to come to an end in 1980 and would have necessitated increasing attention to energy saving measures and some temporary shift in emphasis away from heavy industry. Centrally planned systems regularly run into bottlenecks of this type that force change. There is no reason to think that Chinese central planning couldn't have met the challenge. In fact, it was still in essence a Soviet-style centrally planned industrial system that did meet the challenge in 1980–81.

The slow growth in incomes and consumption also created difficulties. Industrial labor discipline in particular was lax and contributed to industrial inefficiency and even a few strikes. Some workers were even known to disappear from work for a month or longer without being dismissed. But while labor discipline may be the kind of problem that will some day require changes in the economic system of the Soviet Union, it is unlikely that China will face a labor problem of similar magnitude in the next decade or two. There are hundreds of millions of peasants most of whom would gladly trade places with urban factory workers if given the opportunity. If labor discipline got out of hand, a decision could be made to begin to do just that. Even the threat might be enough to get urban labor back to work.

Thus there are ample grounds for believing that China's version of the Soviet economic system could have kept on functioning well into the twenty-first century. Per capita GNP would have continued to grow at 2 or 3 percent a year, perhaps a bit slower or faster depending on luck in finding oil, the degree of political turmoil, and China's external environment. If the system as it was had continued, there would be little point in discussing China as part of the East Asian pattern of growth. The transformation of Chinese society would occur, but only over many decades. China in the year 2000 would still be predominantly a peasant society. The nation's standard of living would be higher but would be much like it is today, a far cry from the levels now prevailing in urbanized South Korea or Taiwan.

CHANGING THE SYSTEM, 1977–1985

But following the death of Mao, the Chinese leadership did not simply retain the system that had evolved over the previous two decades. It began to alter the system often in quite fundamental ways. And as it altered the system, economic

47

growth accelerated to an average of 8 percent a year over the nine years beginning in 1977 and ending in 1985. In that short span of time, as a result, China's gross national product doubled. Per capita national product grew at over 6 percent a year or 75 percent overall. Consumption grew slightly faster because the share of GNP going to capital formation actually declined slightly.

What is it that caused the change? As pointed out in chapter 1, the primary difference between the growth performance of Japan and the East Asian four and that of China was not in the rate of growth of inputs into production. It was the high rate of growth in productivity in the former countries and the lack of it in China that caused the difference. And in China after 1976 accelerated growth was also the result of major increases in productivity. The rate of growth of inputs in China was up little if at all. The share of capital formation in China's GNP actually fell slightly after 1976 although the rate of growth in the capital stock did rise above pre-1976 levels. Labor force growth after 1976 continued at the 2.5 percent a year rate of the previous two decades. Using a similar methodology to that used to calculate productivity growth in Japan and Korea, productivity growth in China after 1976 accounted for half of the GNP growth rate of 8 percent per annum.[3]

The ultimate source of this rise in productivity was the change in political leadership at the top. Mao Zedong, during the last decade and a half of his life, dedicated his energies to creating a new "socialist man" who would work selflessly within a society devoid of class distinctions and motivated by the social good rather than personal material benefits. Mao was not opposed to economic growth, but after the failure of the Great Leap in 1960, he no longer saw social goals as completely consistent with rapid growth in the short run and his clear priority was on the social goals. His wife, Jiang Qing, and the other members of the Shanghai group who played such a key role in carrying out Mao's wishes during the Cultural Revolution, evinced even less interest in economic issues except in so far as they influenced social goals.

China's leadership after 1976, in contrast, placed the pursuit of "wealth and power" for the nation second only to the security and independence of the Chinese state. It has become a convention to date the shift in emphasis to economic growth to the December 1978 Plenum of the Chinese Communist party. But major changes in economic policy were readily apparent even in 1977, a few months after Mao's death and the purge of the "gang of four." The two key changes were in the attitude toward foreign imports and foreign technology and in the role of material incentives in motivating workers. The debate over whether foreign technology was desirable at all was ended decisively in favor of the proposition that imports of such technology were to be actively encouraged. With such encouragement, Chinese enterprises joined the pursuit of foreign goods with enthusiasm and very little restraint. Letters of intent to purchase imports from abroad and even contracts were signed right and left. By the estimate of one Hong Kong firm, Chinese enterprises during those early years of opening up indicated their intention to purchase U.S. $600 billion from abroad, a rather formidable figure given that Chinese exports in those years, the country's main source of foreign exchange, were only U.S. $10 billion per annum.[4] As the experience of 1977–78 indicated, reform would not be a simple process. A major change in one part of the system had implications for many other parts. A Soviet-style system of central planning and administrative controls over the allocation of key inputs, particularly foreign exchange, could not just be opened up and enterprises allowed to purchase abroad in freely convertible domestic currency anything they could afford.

The reintroduction of material incentives into the urban wage system caused fewer problems but also had implications for other parts of the economy. In 1978 the Chinese introduced the first major increase in wages for urban workers in a decade and a half. Equally important, many incentive features in the wage system were restored including promotions from one grade to another, piece rates, and bonuses for good performance. But an increase in wages would be meaningful only if it could be used to purchase items the workers wanted. What they wanted most was better housing, but little new housing had been built in a decade or more and what there was was allocated by administrative means, not through the market. Other consumer goods were also in short supply because of the emphasis on machinery and steel and this emphasis on heavy industry was perpetuated in the ten-year plan reissued in early 1978.

Rather than deal with these inconsistencies by retreating to the known security of Soviet-style central planning, autarky, and heavy industry, the December 1978 Plenum pushed reform a dramatic step forward. Throughout 1979 the changes in policy became public and gained momentum. The shift in emphasis from producer-goods to consumer-goods industry was dictated as much by a growing energy shortage as it was by the need to provide backing for the emphasis on material incentives. The ten-year plan had called for the development of the equivalent of ten new Daqing oil fields. The reality was that there were no immediate prospects for even one new oil field of that size. Petroleum output, which had grown at an average annual rate of 20 percent a year between 1962 and 1978, grew only 2 percent in 1979 and actually fell in 1980.

The immediate solution to this growing energy shortage was to shift emphasis to sectors that made less use of energy, notably consumer goods. The longer term solution was to find more oil and to develop China's known and very large coal resources more rapidly. Toward this latter end, the Chinese government invited foreign oil companies to join it in exploring for oil offshore, a radical departure from a policy that since 1962 had emphasized going it alone without foreign loans of any kind and with little foreign technical assistance. Foreign equity ownership in the past hadn't even been considered.

The introduction of foreign oil companies into the Chinese scene was only one part of a broad-based program to find more sources of foreign exchange. New joint-venture regulations were promulgated (in 1979), designed to encourage foreign direct investment in many fields. China joined the International Monetary Fund and the World Bank and began to borrow from these sources as well as from the export-import banks of Japan and Western Europe. Special economic zones, in essence free trade or export processing zones, were established to encourage exports and the import of advanced technology. A restrictive visa policy that allowed only a few foreigners into China as special guests gave way to a policy of actively promoting foreign tourism. Most importantly, enterprises throughout the country were strongly encouraged to gear more of their production for export. Managers began to pay attention to marketing, a concept alien to central planning where excess demand and captive markets make marketing unnecessary or irrelevant. China's early efforts to sell in the West had their humorous side, such as in the use of the brand name "white elephant" for batteries, but enterprises learned quickly, often with the help of Hong Kong businessmen. In the four years ending in 1982, Chinese exports in U.S. dollar terms grew at 22 percent per year, more than doubling in nominal terms.

The reforms in agriculture were even more dramatic than those in foreign trade and like those in foreign trade, they gathered momentum with each passing year. In the first phase, farmers were encouraged to sell their subsidiary and above-quota products on expanded free markets. In the early 1970s "free" markets, called rural trade fares, existed but often involved a handful of people and few transactions. Driving through the Chinese countryside early in the morning in 1979, one came across gatherings of a thousand people and more engaged in all manner of sales and exchange. By 1985 the state had eliminated or cut way back on quotas for even the major crops, depending instead on market forces to get the produce to where it was needed.

The reform of agricultural production as contrasted to marketing started more slowly. The initial problem was how to reintroduce more material incentives for hard work into the work point systems of the production teams and to lighten the heavy hand of higher level administrative controls over agricultural production management. The barrier to work points allocated on the basis of actual performance was not so much leftist ideology as it was the difficulty and time involved in getting members of a team to sit for long hours debating the merits of each other's work effort. It saved time and avoided strained personal relations to give everyone pretty much the same level of reward per day regardless of the strength, skill, or energy brought to the task. One solution to this tendency was to pay work points on the basis of the completion of defined tasks.

In essence, the "responsibility system," as reform efforts in this area were called, attempted in this way to define tasks and assign small groups or individuals to carry them out. Initially these efforts retained the collective system based on the production team. But assigning defined roles and gearing reward to the completion of those roles, carried to its logical conclusion, involves assigning tasks to individuals or single families. That way a farmer knew that any reward for his or her effort would go to his or her own family, not to other members of the collective group who may or may not have done their share of the work.[5]

By 1982 nearly three-quarters of all farm tasks were being assigned on a household basis and by the summer of 1983 the figure reached 95 percent. Furthermore, assigning particular roles to single households meant in practice that they received an individual plot of land on which to grow the crops they had contracted to produce. The land was assigned to the household for a period of fifteen years, a period that was later extended to encourage more investment in the land. In effect the collective raising of crops had come to an end. China had returned to a system of small family farms similar to that elsewhere in East Asia with the important exception that, in China, land could not be bought or sold.

This reform, from the evidence currently available, was not imposed by the center acting alone. Many Party cadres at the center probably never anticipated that the reforms would go so far and many cadres at lower levels actively resisted the transfer of responsibility for raising grain and other major crops to the household. Such a transfer involved both a loss of power for local cadres and a related reduced ability to carry out the tasks assigned to them. Initially the household-based responsibility system was allowed only in the poorest provinces such as Anhui. Despite cadre resistance, the popularity of the system among farmers led to its rapid spread. Presumably weaker cadres or those less supportive of the collective system allowed the changes first and that put pressure on neighboring cadres to do likewise although currently available evidence isn't sufficient to support this conclusion. What is clear is that the center, led by Deng Xiaoping, first allowed the process to evolve and then stepped in to give the result its formal seal of approval.[6]

The importance of these agricultural reforms for the overall performance of China's economy after 1976 is evidenced by the rise in the rate of growth of the gross value of agricultural output in the six years after 1978 to 9.4 percent per year from an average of 2.9 percent per year over the previous two plus decades. If agriculture (including rural industry) had continued to grow at 2.9 percent through 1984 instead of at the higher rate, the rate of Chinese GNP would have been no more than 6 instead of 8 percent a year and productivity increases would have been less than half the level they actually achieved. All of the other economic reforms combined presumably accounted for the remaining increases in productivity.

Prior to 1985 there were reforms in industry as well as agriculture, but outside of those connected with foreign trade and investment, these industrial reforms are more difficult to appraise. In broad outline industrial reform prior to 1985 involved increasing the decision-making authority of enterprise managers vis-à-vis higher level economic administrators. To that end there was increasing emphasis on profits as contrasted to gross value output as an indicator of success. Investment decisions were also made more and more at lower levels including the enterprise rather than in Beijing. Instead of simply turning over most profits to the center, the system was converted in principle, although not in practice by 1984, to one where enterprises paid in only according to fixed tax rates and kept the rest. There was also an effort to raise the level of competition among enterprises across regions. In earlier years many enterprises in a city such as Chongqing would have a monopoly of the market for their product within the city, the province, or even the entire southwest region. The reforms allowed firms in faraway cities such as Shanghai to sell in those same markets if they could. Since Shanghai quality and technology were generally superior to those of Chongqing, enterprises had to raise quality, lower prices, or make other efforts to meet the competition in certain fields.

For all of these changes, however, the essential features of Soviet-style central planning were still intact in 1984. Key inputs were allocated primarily by administrative means rather than through the market although the share of market-allocated goods had increased. Major investments in new plant and equipment were decided more often than not in Beijing or by provincial-level planners. And enterprises continued to be subjected to a variety of plan targets rather than allowed to maximize profits or decide on their own what targets to pursue as in a capitalist system. Ownership, except for a few joint ventures and many small firms mainly in the countryside, was by the state.

In October 1984 the Chinese Communist party released a sweeping but vaguely worded document calling for further industrial reform. Whether or how that call for reform is likely to be implemented will be discussed below.

### WILL THE REFORMS CONTINUE?

For the purposes of this essay, the central question is whether the reforms begun in the late 1970s will stay in force to a degree necessary to ensure the continuation of China's rapid growth of the past eight or nine years. The assumption behind this question is that reform is necessary for continued growth in productivity and that a reversion to the system in place in the 1960s and 1970s would mean a return to the lower GNP growth rates of that period or worse. There is also the presumption that reform in the Chinese case means moving closer to at least certain key features of the economic strategy and economic system found elsewhere in East Asia. In concrete terms that means retaining an emphasis on an expanding role for foreign trade, household-based agriculture operating in response to market forces, and a substantially enhanced role for the market in industry subject to continued state guidance but not direct control. Failure to reach or maintain this level of reform does not mean that China's economic growth will necessarily grind to a halt or even slow markedly. Growth could continue at a high pace in the absence of further reform or could decelerate even with further reform. Hungary and Yugoslavia, for example, have achieved reforms in their economic systems that go well beyond those currently in force in China in many respects, but no one contemplates 6 to 8 percent growth rates in GNP in those two countries over the next decade or two. The remainder of this chapter, however, will proceed on the assumption that continued reform will help sustain high levels of GNP growth in China.

The prospects for China's economic future can be discussed on two levels. On the first level the issue is whether, in the absence of political change, there are economic forces at work that will alter China's current seemingly bright economic prospects. On the second level the question is whether the political environment will remain supportive of high growth policies. This second level involves much more than simply who will succeed Deng Xiaoping. It includes issues such as whether the reforms themselves will put into play forces that will either build momentum behind further reform or will undo the reforms so far achieved.

Japan, South Korea, Taiwan, and others have demonstrated that GNP growth rates of 8 percent a year and even higher are feasible in the post–World War II era. In terms of per capita income, human resource endowment, level of capital formation, and degree of income inequality China has characteristics similar to those of its East Asian neighbors when they entered into sustained periods of rapid growth. Are there other characteristics that differentiate China from a Korea or a Japan and make its growth prospects dimmer?

The main difference between China and the other nations or territories of East Asia is its size. How does China's enormous size affect the country's economic prospects? One advantage of size is that China, unlike its Asian neighbors, is well-endowed with natural resources. This endowment should put talk of China's energy shortage in perspective. The shortage in the early 1980s was real enough both nationally and regionally. When the Wuhan Iron and Steel Plant was expanded in the mid-1970s, for example, planners failed to take into account the enormous appetite for electric power of the new rolling mills. As it turned out, to run these mills at full capacity, enterprises all over Wuhan had to shut down for lack of power. But the solution to this problem for China is straightforward. The nation needs more electric power plants and needs to drill for more oil and dig for more coal. In the early 1980s China shifted its priorities to do precisely that, with the result that domestic energy supplies, stagnating in 1980 and 1981, grew by over 5 percent in 1982, nearly 7 percent in 1983, and 8 percent or more in 1984 and 1985. China's East Asian neighbors did not have the option of increasing domestic energy production. For them the only question was how much could be imported or saved through energy conservation efforts. For South Korea and Taiwan in the early 1980s, petroleum imports alone accounted for 20 to 25 percent of the total import bill. For China petroleum was a small but significant earner of foreign exchange.

Another implication of large size that may be less favorable to China is that large countries typically have much lower trade ratios than small countries, that is, they depend on foreign trade less. China, therefore, may not enjoy the same gains from trade as the others where trade was a much larger share of GNP. It was easier for those nations to specialize on those products they could manufacture best and import the rest. Producing for export also instilled the discipline of international competition into Korea's and Taiwan's industries. Chinese enterprises producing for export are also benefiting from these stimuli, but there are fewer such enterprises relative to those that produce for the domestic market. Whatever the merits of this argument, however, it shouldn't be carried too far. China's trade ratio in the 1980s is roughly the same as that of Japan prior to the OPEC rise in oil prices in 1973. Most of the Japanese economy produced goods and services for the Japanese domestic market and Japan still managed to achieve large gains in productivity.

The main danger for China on the international trade front is that world markets may not grow as fast or remain as open as in the 1950s and 1960s. Creeping protectionism poses a very real threat to exporters of manufactures, but does this mean that China's export drive is doomed to failure? China's exports in the early 1980s were just over 1 percent of the world total leaving considerable room for expansion before China is seen as "another Japan." Many Chinese exports compete not so much for new markets in the United States and

Europe as against products now supplied by Korea, Taiwan, or Hong Kong where wages are now far higher than in China. In addition, where import restrictions do apply to Chinese goods in Japan and the United States, China's bargaining position is by no means weak, for political and strategic reasons if no other. In short, it is difficult to construct a convincing case that external economic forces will limit China's export drive and slow growth overall. Whether or not internal forces will slow export growth will be dealt with in a moment.

Finally, there is the question of Chinese agriculture. The rapid growth of Chinese agriculture in the 1979–84 period and the advent of grain surpluses too large for domestic granaries induced a brief sense of euphoria among some analysts of the Chinese economy, both outside and particularly inside China. The sharp drop in grain output in 1985 should reintroduce a clearer sense of China's long-term agricultural prospects. Like the rest of East Asia, China must feed a great many people on very little land. Japan, South Korea, and Taiwan have all solved this problem by increasingly relying on imports of food, particularly grain. But can China, with its enormous population, rely more and more heavily on imports of grain? If China were to import as much grain per capita as Korea in 1981, for example, China would have to import over 180 million tons of grain. World grain prices would rise sharply and China's foreign exchange reserves would fall, even if China's foreign exchange earnings continue to grow rapidly over the next decade or two.

Thus, China's size and the resulting lower foreign trade ratio suggest that China must invest heavily enough in agriculture to keep domestic agricultural production at a level sufficient to prevent imports of food from becoming too large. What constitutes "too large" will depend on how fast

Chinese exports of manufactures grow, on the rate of growth of grain output in surplus countries, and on the productivity of investments in agriculture and agricultural research among other things. On balance, however, China's need to limit food imports below the shares of its East Asian neighbors probably makes it more difficult for China to achieve comparable rates of growth in overall productivity. Despite the experience of the early 1980s, productivity growth rates in Chinese agriculture over the next decade or two, like those elsewhere in East Asia, are not likely to be as high as in industry.

### POLITICS, REFORM, AND FUTURE GROWTH

A central theme of both of these essays is that sustained rapid growth depends most of all on a supportive political environment. That was the case with China's East Asian neighbors in the past and it was the crucial element in China's own accelerated growth after 1976. Any forecast of China's economic future, therefore, must deal with the question of whether the nation's political environment will remain supportive of economic growth and growth-oriented policies over the next decade or two.

The question is usually posed in terms of what happens after Deng Xiaoping relinquishes the reins of power. Who will his successors be and will they continue his policies? To answer these questions one must begin with some understanding of how the Chinese Communist party picks its leaders.

Leadership of the Chinese state is determined by the Communist party, and leadership of the party is decided by a small group of people at the top of the party hierarchy, basically the Chinese Politburo and its Standing Committee. Within the Politburo certain individuals have more influence than others and at times a single individual such as Mao Zedong can dominate the selection of new members and the decisions of the body. Mao's dominance, like that of Deng Xiaoping in the 1980s, rested as much or more on those individuals' support and following within the broader ranks of the party and the army, not just on support within the Politburo itself. In the absence of a champion within the Politburo, however, even quite large factions within the broad ranks of the party and army will have little influence on major policy decisions or on the political succession. In the mid-1980s central power rested as much with the Party Secretariat as with the Politburo, but the essential point is the same. Decision-making on important issues in China is highly centralized. Participatory democratic processes whereby the broad mass of party members picks their leaders simply do not exist in China.

Because of this political structure, change in policy in China comes about as a result of either a change in leadership at the top or a changing of minds on the part of the existing top leadership or some combination of the two. If such a change does occur, policies can be altered in major ways in a short period of time, because the system does not require a slow process of consensus-building prior to instituting even radical shifts in policy. On the other hand, if the central leadership is unified behind a set of policies, those policies are not likely to change.

In the early 1970s the top leadership was deeply split on a wide range of policy issues affecting the economy. By the late 1970s the range of the debate had narrowed, but the differences between those around Deng Xiaoping and those around Ye Jianying and Hua Guofeng were still substantial. By the mid-1980s both Ye and Hua were out of the top leadership and policy differences at the top had narrowed further. The main source of opposition to some of the new policies, particularly those involved in opening up to the West, was Chen Yun, an architect of Chinese economic policy in the 1950s and early 1960s, but a man past eighty years of age in 1985. Most of the rest of the Politburo and all of the Party Secretariat were made up of individuals associated with the reforms. At lower levels of the party and within the army and the state bureaucracy, Deng and his followers have orchestrated a systematic if bloodless transfer to a new generation of leaders, better trained than their predecessors and, so far as the top leadership was in a position to judge, committed to reform.

Given this political situation, are major changes in economic policy likely or even possible over the next decade or two? Certainly it is difficult to picture an elderly Chen Yun leading a purge of the current leadership and a reversion to earlier policies.[7] Even if he had the desire to do this, which is unlikely, he has neither the power base nor the time required. If there is to be a change in leadership and policy, therefore, it is likely to come after Deng Xiaoping has passed from the scene and there is a falling out among his successors.

But who among Deng's successors is going to build a power base on a platform opposed to the current reforms? All have been picked in part because of their association with and support for those reforms. Central opposition to the reforms, therefore, most likely will have to come from a former reformer who for one reason or another has become disillusioned with reform. Such an individual could be an opportunist attempting to build a power base among the discontented ranks of the party and the army. Or someone who had genuinely come to feel that the reforms were not working or at least were causing more trouble than they were worth.

### FORCES UNDERMINING REFORM

What could cause an active reformer today to conclude that the reform was a failure and had to be reversed? The most obvious case would be if these reforms failed to maintain accelerated growth. Part of the momentum behind reform in the mid-1980s was the evidence of successful results that were there for all to see. This evidence was particularly apparent in the case of agriculture. The Chinese Communist party probably has the power to reverse the agricultural reforms and restore collectivized agriculture, but is any Chinese leader likely to try? The effort would almost certainly lead to a decline in agricultural productivity and the rate of growth in the rural standard of living and possibly an absolute fall in that standard. Would ideological preferences for the old commune system plus a desire for greater political control over the countryside associated with collectivization justify taking such a risk with the rural standard of living and the nation's food supply? If Mao Zedong were still in charge the answer probably would be yes, but no one in the current leadership appears to share a similar vision for China's future.

More likely is that a consensus could build among the current leadership that reform was causing excessive inflation, rising levels of corruption, and increases in inequality. The inflationary pressures of 1985 have already caused rising resentment among China's urban population. After the experience with hyperinflation in the 1940s followed by three decades when prices hardly moved at all, the Chinese people have a low tolerance for price increases even if it is demonstrable that they are accompanied by marked rises in their real standard of living. The problem appears to be concentrated in the cities, because farmers are more the beneficiaries than the victims of rising prices. Some of the increases are temporary. Beijing, for example, apparently tried to solve its growing traffic problem by banning transport of vegetables into the city except by farmers resident within the Beijing district. The result was skyrocketing vegetable prices and a quick decision to allow in vegetables from more distant rural areas after all. But there are also long-term sources of inflationary pressure that are being brought into the open by the reforms. With prices frozen, individuals often had more money than they could use and so put it in the bank. The only way to get goods in short supply was to get in a queue or use the "back door." Some goods are still subject to long waiting lists, but more and more are available for a price, particularly food products.

Decentralization of decision-making authority to the enterprises has also meant bonuses and other wage increases in excess of available consumer supplies, hence pressure on prices. Eventually all of these pressures may be brought under control by more effective management of macroeconomic variables, but that degree of effectiveness is not likely to be achieved soon. In the meantime urban consumers will continue to criticize higher prices and blame the reforms. Some may even prefer to return to the period of shortages and long waiting lines, but many will simply criticize inflation and enjoy the benefits of more and better goods, conveniently available, without really understanding the connection between the two.

The problems of corruption and inequality are in some ways interrelated and probably a greater inherent danger to the future of the reforms. For nearly three decades China's leaders extolled the virtues of working selflessly for the common good. Party members, in particular, were expected to live by those principles. In reality senior officials, including party cadres, were paid substantially higher wages than ordinary workers and received other special privileges, and ordinary urban workers themselves enjoyed a much higher standard of living than most people in the countryside. But the special privileges of the elite were largely hidden from view behind the closely guarded gates of Zhongnanhai in Beijing and other similar places where the elite lived. Conspicuous consumption was a formula for personal political eclipse. Those without political power basically lacked the means to get rich. Economic power in China's fully socialized urban society and collectivized rural society was in the hands of those with political power.

By the mid-1980s, in contrast, individuals were encouraged to get rich and the burgeoning private and collective sector gave some the means to do so. Party cadres were still supposed to remain aloof from such activities, but now they had to sit back and watch while others with less influence and power built new homes and bought color television sets. Some, perhaps many, gave in to the temptation to turn political power into economic gain.

One of the problems with corruption in a highly controlled society such as China's is that it is difficult to define. Soviet-style central planning regularly requires the trading of favors between enterprises. The plan is always full of mistakes and these mistakes are rectified by one enterprise trading its surplus supplies to make up for shortages in the planned allocation of other inputs. The process is built on personal relationships (*guanxi*), because these inputs are not available on any market. Formally the process is illegal, but the system would grind to a halt in its absence. Those who are skilled at making these arrangements have enterprises that meet and pass their plan targets and they get promoted or are rewarded in other ways.

When does this process of mutual favors become corrup

tion? There is no easy answer. The extreme cases, to be sure, are straightforward. An official in charge of issuing licenses who does so only after receiving money under the table is corrupt in any system. But criticism of officials in China who are getting rich is not confined to those who receive bribes. In the eyes of some party members, almost any party member who receives and enjoys material benefits too much is suspect, even if the benefits are received through legal channels. Some of this criticism is based on simple envy, as is the case when urban residents speak of rural people who are becoming richer than they are. But there is also the belief among many of the party that party members, at least, should set a personal standard of austerity and personal sacrifice that is inconsistent with "getting rich" by whatever means.

Even more complicated are the situations where cadres manipulate the system to benefit their units rather than themselves. The Hainan authorities who bought foreign exchange on the black market and used it to import low duty or duty free automobiles and color televisions for resale throughout China are a case in point. While the individuals involved received personal rewards, the main beneficiaries of the enormous profits earned were their units. Their principal crime was that they cost the Chinese state over a billion dollars in foreign exchange by their manipulations. If the cost had been only a few hundred thousand or even a few million dollars, what these officials did might have received only mild criticism, if any at all. Buying foreign exchange on the black market was clearly illegal, but their ability to buy so much is itself testimony to how widespread was the practice of illegally buying and selling foreign exchange.

In a capitalist society where controls are few, individuals are expected to use their ingenuity to increase their wealth. Any transaction on a legal market is legitimate whether the benefits of the transaction are spread widely or narrowly. These markets are subject to legal rules and restrictions, and violation of those rules and restrictions is a prosecutable offense. Economic success, however, does not normally require that an individual or an enterprise break the rules. Society has little difficulty in defining such rule breaches as illegitimate and prosecuting the offenders. When the offenders are public officials it is called corruption, although the term applies to certain activities in the private sector as well.

But in China, as already pointed out, individuals and enterprises must make their way through a minefield of complex and often contradictory rules and regulations. Success is achieved, not by rigid adherence to the rules, but by careful selection of which rules to follow and which to ignore. The legitimacy of this approach is reinforced by the weakness of China's own legal tradition, but the problems are inherent to socialist central planning or any economy that relies extensively on direct government controls over the economy. Corruption in such a system becomes a highly subjective concept. Its meaning depends on the values of those who hold power in China. In the hands of leaders who share Chen Yun's concern with the "infiltration of decadent capitalist ideology and its work style," anti-corruption campaigns could become weapons against the economic reforms themselves.

### THE COMPLEXITY OF URBAN REFORM

Perhaps the greatest danger to the reform process, however, is not inflation or corruption, but the very complexity of the process. That complexity means that mistakes in implementing reform are inevitable. Any mistakes will lead to setbacks in the economy that will undermine political support for further reform.

Why is the process so complex? The reason is that the movement from a system involving central planning and administrative allocation of inputs to one which makes substantially greater use of market forces involves several essential and interrelated steps. Failure to implement one of these steps can undermine the effectiveness of the others.

What are the crucial steps required to make a market-based system work efficiently? In essence there are five kinds of change or reform required, three of which are absolutely essential, and the other two highly desirable.

1. Goods must be made available for purchase and sale on the market, including a high proportion of intermediate inputs for state enterprises. If inputs are not freely available for purchase and sale, enterprise managers will continue to spend most of their energy on attempting to influence the central plan and those controlling the administrative allocation of essential products. In effect, enterprise managers will remain low-level bureaucrats carrying out the orders of those above them in the hierarchy. Real enterprise autonomy in decision-making will not have been achieved.

2. But simply making products available through markets will lead to major misallocation of inputs if the prices of those products do not reflect relative scarcities in the economy. Chinese prices of industrial inputs have been frozen, often for two decades or more. Those prices, to the extent that they reflect scarcities at all, reflect conditions that existed in the early 1950s when China's industrial economy was one-twentieth of its size in the mid-1980s. Major price reform is essential but difficult to implement. Does a central authority set out to measure the marginal cost of each item available for purchase and sale? Or does it simply make the goods available and let prices float until they find their equilibrium price?

This latter method will lead to chaos if little progress has been made on the third essential step.

3. The third step is to ensure that enterprise managers and others involved in the purchase and sale of products behave in accordance with the rules of the market. In essence, they must maximize enterprise profits or follow some rule that is a reasonable approximation of profit maximization. If enterprises maximize profits they will attempt to cut back on the use of inputs whose prices have risen and make greater use of inputs whose prices have fallen. Similarly, they will shift their product mix toward items whose prices are rising and away from those that are falling.

If, on the other hand, enterprise managers continue to attempt to maximize gross value output and to ignore profits and the cost of inputs, the market won't work. The 1977–78 and 1984–85 runs on foreign exchange illustrate what happens under such circumstances. Authority to purchase inputs abroad was given to lower level authorities and they immediately began a major expansion of foreign purchases; foreign exchange reserves fell, and central controls were quickly reestablished. Further devaluation of the Chinese currency would have helped stem the tide of purchases, but without a fundamental change in the rules governing enterprise behavior, the devaluation would have had to have been a massive one.

Reform in the rural areas was much easier to implement, because it was much easier to achieve these three steps in the countryside. The third step was attained when decision-making was turned over to the individual household. Farm households are natural profit or income maximizers since their welfare depends on following such a goal. Even production team leaders are more natural profit maximizers than enterprise managers, since there is a clear relationship between the welfare of the team and the degree to which it maximizes its income, unlike in industry. Prices and markets were also easier to free up in the rural areas, because a significant fraction of agricultural produce was already being sold on markets where prices were allowed to fluctuate before 1985.

Even in the rural areas, however, the introduction of market forces has had its problems, in part because of difficulties in implementing one of the other two steps needed for truly efficient reform.

4. Macroeconomic controls over the economy must be well managed. If decontrol leads to price increases that are then matched by large wage increases, an inflationary spiral can be set off. With large pent-up demand left over from decades of price control, inflationary pressures in the initial phases of reform are inevitable. The question is, what happens after that? Will inflation continue because the government either doesn't understand how to stop it, or, more likely, lacks the political will to bring it to an end by capping wages of urban workers for a time?

5. The fifth step involves the elimination of monopolies in the purchase and sale of products. Markets will lead to major gains in efficiency only if there is vigorous competition. In China prior to the 1980s, enterprises tended to be given monopolies in particular regions. Even county-level enterprises had a monopoly over the market in their own county and restrictions on their ability to sell in the markets of other counties.

By mid-1985 China had made some progress in bringing about change in all of these five areas.[8] Competition was introduced for enterprises, particularly in the commercial sphere, but also in the production of some consumer goods and industrial inputs. The role of the profits target was enhanced by measures connecting profits to worker bonuses and to other small investments of interest to plant managers. The proportion of goods available for purchase and sale on the market has increased markedly. A dual price system for goods allocated within and without the plan has been created. Within-plan prices have changed little, but products bought and sold outside of the plan often fetch much higher prices that come closer to reflecting those products' value to society. The government also recognized that it needs to do a much better job in the area of macroeconomic management, but its efforts to stem inflation have been ad hoc and not very effective.

In summary, China's leadership is making a real and sustained effort to reform the economic system. The system that existed in 1985, however, was still an uncomfortable mix of Soviet-style central planning with elements of market socialism. The complexity of running such a system leads to mistakes, and mistakes, if serious enough, can undermine the reforms. On the other hand, by the mid-1980s, there was little reason for believing that the reforms had lost their momentum. Nor on balance, in my opinion, is there likely to be a loss of momentum in the immediate future or over the longer term. If that belief is valid, then there is every reason to assume that rapid growth in China will continue. Rapid growth in this context means an annual average increase in GNP of 6 to 8 percent over the next decade and a half or more.

Continued rapid growth may not be realized, but if it is, the impact of growth on the Chinese economy and Chinese society will be profound. China in the mid-1980s is on the edge of a major transition away from its rural peasant origins. How it handles that transition in the next decade will shape China's social and economic future well into the twenty-first

71

century. Some of the major choices that China will face are the subject of the remainder of this essay.

Gross national product growth rates of 6 to 8 percent a year for China translate into per capita increases of 4.5 to 6.5 percent annually if population continues to grow at current levels of 1.5 percent a year. The Chinese leadership would like to see this population growth rate fall further, but the one-child family policy by 1985 was already increasingly perceived as too draconian to be sustained. A fully implemented one-child family policy, as demographers have been pointing out, would lead in the twenty-first century to a situation where a small number of working age people, the former single children, would be supporting a very high ratio of non-working adults, their elderly parents. It would be the reverse of the current situation where a large number of working age people, the products of the population explosion of the 1950s and 1960s, are supporting a small number of retirees. In addition, the single-child policy could lead to a marked distortion in the sex ratio because of the strong East Asian preference for male offspring. Hospitals in Seoul, Korea, in 1985, for example, reported a male-female ratio in new births of 1.17 to 1.0, leading the government to ban ultrasonic and other medical tests designed to ascertain the sex of a fetus during pregnancy.[9] And Korea's family planning efforts are completely voluntary. For all of these reasons and others, China is likely to relax the one-child policy and, in fact, has already begun to do so.

If growth rates in per capita income of 4.5 to 6.5 per year are attained, China's per capita income, which was between $300 and $500 in the mid-1980s would rise to anywhere from

$600 to over $1,200. For my purpose here, a narrower range of $800 to $1,000 in 1985 prices, the most likely outcome, will be used. If realized, these figures imply that China will essentially duplicate the growth experience of Korea in the 1960s. What will take China fifteen years to accomplish occurred in Korea and Taiwan in slightly less time, but in all three countries or regions the period of transition to the middle income society was or will be extremely rapid by historical standards.

In chapter 1 the implications of this rise in per capita income for how people in the Republic of Korea and in Taiwan live was explored. Will China's experience be the same or are there reasons for anticipating major differences?

## URBANIZATION AND OFF-FARM EMPLOYMENT

Historically, an increase in per capita income from $400 to $800-$1,000 has been accompanied by a marked shift in employment out of agriculture and into industry and services. On average the drop in the share of agricultural (and mining) employment has been from over 60 percent to under 50 percent[10] and the farm employment shares of Korea and Taiwan, as noted earlier, followed a path similar to that of the rest of the world. Along with this shift in employment went an even more rapid change in the residence of the population as a whole. For all nations, the share of those residing in urban areas rose from just over 20 percent of total population to just under 40 percent.[11] The Republic of Korea and Taiwan, however, began their period of rapid growth with over 40 percent of their people in urban areas and this figure leaped above 60 percent in the 1970s.

How does China fit into this pattern of rapid urbanization and growth in off-farm employment? To begin with, China, even in 1984, still had 72 percent of its labor force in agriculture. By any standard China in 1984 was still a rural society, but was this rural orientation the natural outcome of the level of development of the Chinese economy or a product of deliberate policies designed to restrict the growth of cities and off-farm employment?

That China has made a major effort to limit urbanization is not in question. In fact, foreign observers have frequently applauded these efforts as a means of avoiding the rapid expansion of the slums and shanty-towns found in so many other urban areas in developing countries. The main vehicles used to accomplish this end were a series of regulations and actions designed to make rural to urban migration nearly impossible. Permits were required to leave one's rural commune and another permit was required to stay even a few days in the city. In the absence of an urban residence permit, an individual was not eligible to receive grain ration coupons. Enterprises were not supposed to hire directly, but through labor bureaus, and these bureaus sought to meet this demand among people who already resided in urban areas. As a result, while employment in state-owned and urban collective and individual units rose nearly fivefold from 25 million persons in 1952 to 117 million in 1983, the urban population rose just over threefold from 72 million in 1952 to 241 million in 1983.[12]

Part of this difference, however, is a statistical artifact. In 1984 China changed the criteria for determining urban towns and the urban population jumped to 330 million, 31.9 percent of total population.[13] If this figure stands up, then China's efforts to restrict urbanization may not have had as much impact as commonly supposed except in a few major urban centers such as Shanghai. In the areas immediately surrounding "officially" designated urban areas was a large population, nearly 90 million people, most of whom were urban in everything but name. Some of these 90 million, however, still raised vegetables and performed other agricultural tasks.

My concern, however, is with the future and, for that purpose, whether China's urban population rose from 12.5 to 31.9 percent of the total between 1952 and 1984 or by some lesser amount is not the issue. The question is whether that ratio will continue to rise in the future and at what rate. If China's urban population continues to grow at the nearly 5 percent per annum rate of the past three decades, China's urban population by the year 2000 will double to 660 million people, or over 50 percent of China's total. An increase of 330 million new residents in the urban population in fifteen years is huge, but as a change in population share, it is no different from what happened in Korea or Taiwan or, for that matter, much of the rest of the developing world, where per capita incomes rose two and a half times from a base of $300 or $500.

Will such an increase really take place? The World Bank in its 1985 report assumes a GNP growth rate per capita of 4.3 to 5.5 percent, not markedly different from the projections used here. But the Bank economists project that the urban share in the total will rise by only five to ten percentage points and, in one of their scenarios, will not rise at all.[14] Under the most rapid urban development projection they present, the number of people in cities rises at only 3 percent a year, substantially *slower* than the 5 percent a year figure used above, or the 4 percent per annum figure derived from official Chinese data before the redefinition of the urban population in 1984. In effect, the Bank economists are assuming that the Chinese government will be able to restrict urban growth to a level even below that achieved by the very restrictive policies of the past.

While tight control of rural to urban migration under conditions of rapid industrialization might be possible, is there any reason to think such restrictions are desirable? These policies in the past had the effect of widening the rural-urban income gap. They may also have led to the increasing capital intensity of Chinese industry, although cause and effect is difficult to prove in this case. In effect, Chinese policy had much to do with creating a dual economic structure, where a modernizing capital-intensive urban population lived alongside a separate and much poorer rural population, whose workers still moved rock and dirt with shovels, baskets, and strong backs. Those born into these rural areas, especially those who lived a long distance from a major city, could expect to spend the rest of their lives in the same village.

The gain to the state from these restrictive policies was a substantial savings on investment in urban infrastructure. In fact, investment in housing did not keep up with urban population growth, and the floor space per capita fell to 3.6 square meters in 1978.[15] On a psychological and political level, urban residents were also spared the unpleasantness of having to live near squatters with their poor sanitation and higher rates of crime. Foreign and Chinese observers alike have suggested that preventing urban squalor in this way was really in the interests of those who would make up the urban poor, but surveys around the world show that few of the urban poor would agree. They invariably consider themselves better off in these urban slums than they were back in their villages. If they didn't consider themselves better off, they would have returned to the countryside long ago.

Does the cost of urban infrastructure justify continued efforts to sharply curtail urban growth? Current levels of urban infrastructure investment are necessary to overcome a decade and more of neglect. Future urban growth, particularly if roughly 300 million more people enter the cities over the next decade and a half, will require continued high levels of investment in housing, sanitation, and transport. But this "non productive" investment, to use the Chinese term, does not require many imported inputs and so should be feasible. Urban housing, for example, would have to average 18 billion yuan a year, perhaps 20 percent of the total state investment in capital construction over the same period, about the same amount spent on housing in the early 1980s.[16]

The alternative is to try to keep most of the people in the rural areas. If keeping them in the rural areas means retaining them in agricultural employment, that is the same as condemning these people to low and comparatively stagnant incomes. The spurt in agricultural production in the 1979–84 period was, as already indicated, a one-shot phenomenon connected with overcoming the inefficiency of collectivized agriculture. Per capita crop output will continue to grow, but not at a rate sufficient to raise per capita farm incomes by 4.5 to 6.5 percent a year, the national average rate of increase in per capita GNP, while the farm population is itself growing at 1 percent a year.

Furthermore, whatever the precise rate of agricultural growth, achieving it is unlikely to require a rural workforce of 350 million, growing at 5 million workers or more a year with under 0.3 of a hectare per worker.[17] China, with its large machine-building capacity, is in a position at modest cost to mechanize many agricultural tasks and make an even larger share of China's agricultural workforce "surplus." Agricultural employment per hectare of cultivated land in Taiwan fell to 0.49 hectares per capita in 1963 and 1964, and then began rising as the agricultural workforce began to fall. The low point for South Korea was just over 0.4 hectares per worker. China is already well below either level and still falling. No doubt additional farm workers could find some kind of productive employment, but not employment that would lead to rapid and sustained increases in per capita income and consumption. Clearly it is time for China to make a major effort to move large numbers of workers away from raising crops to other occupations.

Fewer and fewer Chinese would dispute the logic of the above argument, but many still hope that people can be moved out of agriculture without having to allow them to migrate to cities. The Chinese even have a slogan for this policy, "to leave the land, but not to leave the countryside" (*li tu bu li xiang*).[18] The method of achieving this goal is rural industrialization.

Sideline production, most of which is rural industry, grew at an average annual rate of 20 percent during the six years, 1979 to 1984. But for all this growth, in 1984 only 10.3 million people were employed by rural collective industries. Even if one adds employees of those few state-owned industries that are located outside of cities, it is clear that rural industry would have to continue to grow at its current high rate for some time before rural industry would absorb a large share of just the projected increase in the rural workforce.

Furthermore, there are good reasons why industrial enterprises historically have located close together, thus forming cities. These enterprises require large and regular sources of electric power, and a good transport system to move goods to and away from their factories, plus many other kinds of infrastructure. In the early stages of development it is usually most efficient to concentrate this infrastructure rather than scatter it evenly across the countryside.

Much of China's recent rural industrialization is, in fact, really an extension of the country's urban industrial program. Some 50 percent of all collective industry employment, both rural and urban, is concentrated in five provinces and three directly controlled cities. The remaining twenty-one provinces with 75 percent of the population have the rest. If more refined regional data were available, they would no doubt show that even in these industrially more developed provinces along the coast, collective industry was unevenly distributed. In Jiangsu, for example, rural industry was heavily concentrated in the southern part of the province in a belt stretching from Shanghai through the cities of Suzhou and Wuxi to Nanjing. Factories in the large cities increasingly subcontract activities to neighboring rural areas as a way around restrictions on their ability to hire more labor or to acquire additional land for expansion. This process will no doubt continue, but it has more the character of urban-industrial expansion than it does that of dispersed rural industrialization. The great majority of the population in the countryside will see little of this kind of rural industrialization.

If there is no real substitute for urbanization in China over the next fifteen years and beyond, there are real choices about how urbanization is to be accomplished. In most countries urbanization has occurred in response to economic forces and policies made with little concern for their impact on the urban development process. The same condition may arise in China, but the government's active effort to control the growth of cities in the past suggests that the potential for an alternative to unplanned urbanization exists.

What are the principal choices? The central questions are: How many people should be allowed to leave the rural areas for the cities, and which of the 700 million still in the countryside should be the ones chosen to move?

If a poll were taken among China's urban residents, it is likely that a substantial majority would support continued tight restrictions on new entrants to the cities. Investment in housing, in this view, should be used to relieve existing overcrowding, not to spread the overcrowding over a larger number of people. But this view is unrealistic on both economic and political grounds. On economic grounds, rapid industrialization accompanied by the development of ancillary services will require large numbers of new workers. Labor-saving technology can reduce the number required, but will make industrial investment more expensive than necessary. On the political side, such policies would exacerbate the dual nature of China's development program condemning hundreds of millions of rural youth, many who are talented and ambitious, to a future with little hope for significant advancement for themselves or even their children. Would the Chinese Communist party and the People's Liberation Army, both of whose roots go deep into the countryside, allow this to happen?

The more interesting question, therefore, is not whether large numbers of people will move to the cities, but who it is that will be permitted to change their residence. The current policy draws most new urban workers from the rural areas immediately surrounding the cities. But this policy has already stripped suburban farms around the major cities of most of their adult male workers, leaving farming to women and children. Future migrants will have to come from farther afield, where it is no longer so easy to work in the cities while living in the countryside and commuting between the two on a regular basis. Even if existing practices can be maintained for another decade and beyond, they have the undesirable effect of making already rich suburban farm families even richer, while leaving more distant areas unaffected. Control over rural to urban migration has been the single greatest cause of increasing inequality in recent years, and continuation of those controls will exacerbate the problem further.

An alternative variation on the current policy would be to

allow only the workers themselves to migrate, bringing them in from more distant areas and putting them up in dormitories. But this policy means that tens of millions of Chinese laborers would in effect be "guest workers" in their own country, much like the Turks and Yugoslavs in German industry. The policy would save on investment in urban infrastructure, but would it be politically feasible once the numbers became large? It seems unlikely.

If families are to be allowed to migrate to the cities, how will they be selected and which cities will they go to? Current policy is to emphasize the development of smaller more dispersed towns rather than existing large cities, but that policy will make sense only if the necessary infrastructure can be built at acceptable cost. If not, urban enterprises in all cities will search the surrounding countryside for workers and then scramble to find housing for them and their families.

An alternative would be for the central government to give priority for migration to rural people from the poorest areas such as Gansu and Guizhou provinces. The Chinese government does have a program to move these people from poorer to richer farming areas, but not many poor people can be accommodated in this way in a country that has little developable arable land other than that already under cultivation.[19]

This is not the place to attempt to spell out an optimal policy for China over the next decade or two. The point is that China will have to find some way to move as many as 300 million people. How it does this will affect the fundamental nature of Chinese society and the future of the reform effort itself. At one extreme, China in the year 2000 will be a society with rising inequality between urban and rural areas and with 70 percent of the population still resident in the countryside, although not necessarily employed there. At the other extreme is a society which is 50 percent urban, where inequality has been reduced by selective migration from the poorest areas.

### THE IMPACT OF CONSUMER DURABLES

Urbanization is only one part of the fundamental change in life style that occurs when a nation's per capita income rises 2½-fold to around 1,000 dollars. There are also marked shifts in consumption patterns. Some of these shifts involve increases in the amount of meat in the diet, more stylish clothing, and larger and better-built housing in rural as well as urban areas.

Some changes in consumption patterns have a political and social impact that can be profound. This is particularly true of certain consumer durables, notably television sets and automobiles. The automobile revolution in personal mobility won't occur in China until well into the twenty-first century and so it will not be dealt with here. But the television revolution is already well underway. Roughly 30 percent of all urban households have TV sets and the percentage of the population that watches television either at work, with neighbors, or in some neighborhood unit is much larger. TV aerials also sprout above the roofs of rural villages in the vicinity of cities. Walking down a Chinese street at eight or nine o'clock in the evening, one finds family after family gathered around the television.

It is easy for an American brought up with television and with easy access to many sources of information to underestimate the impact of this phenomenon. Only ten years ago the Chinese press and radio could tell the Chinese people that their East Asian neighbors lived in societies that were mostly poor with a few rich exploiters. Then the Chinese people were shown pictures of Japan as it really was when Deng Xiaoping and later other leaders visited the country. Japan's high technology prosperity was a shock to many of those watching.

Unlike the theater, with television one can't show the same performance over and over again and expect anyone to continue watching. For ten years Chinese had little to watch other than a handful of "revolutionary operas" approved by Jiang Qing. A similar limited fare in the age of television is conceivable, but not very likely. Cultural czars still control what the Chinese public is allowed to see, but complete control is harder to achieve if one is also under pressure to produce meaningful entertainment and education night after night.

The other sources of new and uncontrolled information flowing into China include the tens of thousands of Chinese students sent abroad and now returning, the millions of overseas Chinese with their relatives in the Southeast, Beijing and Shanghai, and hundreds of thousands of other foreign tourists, businessmen, scholars, and students.

In summary, a fundamental change in Chinese society is underway affecting how people live and, of comparable importance, how they think. The impact is much greater in the urban areas and along China's coast than it is in the rural areas in the country's interior. This coastal-interior, urban-rural dichotomy is an old one in modern Chinese history. In the past when the two sides have clashed, more often than not it was the rural interior values that came out on top. If rapid growth over the next fifteen years leads to a major improvement in the standard of living and a large-scale transfer of population to the cities, traditional peasant values may finally have been put on the defensive permanently.

These two essays began with a discussion of the historically unprecedented rates of growth achieved in parts of East Asia since the end of World War II. This achievement, it was argued, was the result of a favorable human resource endowment combined with a supportive political environment which included outward-oriented economic policies. The accelerated economic development that this combination of forces made possible led to a transformation of East Asian society. While many traditional values were retained, those values had to be applied in a completely new environment, one that was more urban than rural, where individuals were being constantly bombarded by the material goods, ideas, and values of the world beyond East Asia. The isolated, tradition-bound peasant societies of Japan, the Republic of Korea, Taiwan, Hong Kong, and Singapore no longer exist.

This second essay has attempted to show how China started with a similar human resource endowment as the rest of East Asia, but from a lower per capita income base in 1949 and a very different set of economic policies. By 1977 or 1979, however, China's per capita income had reached a level comparable to that of Korea or Taiwan in the 1950s and a dramatic change in China's economic policies brought them closer to those of the country's East Asian neighbors, with notable differences. The most important difference was China's retention of state socialism and many of the trappings of central planning. Despite the retention of state ownership and more planning than existed elsewhere in East Asia, China's growth rate rose to an East Asian-style level of 8 percent a year and the country's GNP doubled between 1977 and 1985.

Whether these unprecedented rates of growth will continue in East Asia including China is partly a question of external forces shaping the international economic system, but of much greater importance is whether East Asia's own political environment will remain supportive of the policies that have done so well by the region to date. In the Republic of Korea the main issue is how to achieve a stable and constitutional transition from one government to another. In Hong Kong and eventually in Taiwan the issue is how to reach some kind of an accommodation with the government of the People's Republic of China. The major question mark over the next decade, however, is over what will happen in China itself when that huge nation begins its transition to a new leadership. I have pointed out here some of the pitfalls that stand in the way of a smooth transition, but also have suggested that the momentum toward reform will be difficult to derail.

If the political environment does remain supportive, there is every reason to believe that China will undergo an economic and social transformation with many features similar to those that occurred elsewhere in East Asia. If this change does take place, one-quarter of the world's population will have moved in the latter half of the twentieth century from a closed, poor, rural, peasant society to a society where living standards are rising rapidly, where the dominant share of the population is increasingly urban and industrial, and where the nations of the region are fully integrated into the international economic system. Few if any events in the last half of the twentieth century are of comparable significance either to the people of East Asia or to the rest of us.

APPENDIX

# The Measurement of
# East Asian Productivity

The term "productivity" can take on several different meanings. One common measure of productivity, for example, is the amount of output or income per worker. Increases in output per worker, however, can arise either because of the increasing efficiency of that worker or because the worker has greater amounts of other inputs, notably capital, with which to work. In these essays the interest is in increases in the productivity of all inputs taken together, not just that of labor. Thus the relevant measure is "total factor productivity." One measure of "total factor productivity" is the "residual" output remaining after subtracting increases in output, or income accounted for by increases in inputs such as capital and labor. The technique is called "growth accounting" or "sources of growth analysis."

In some instances, inputs are defined broadly to include such things as increases in the education level of the work force. Inputs, as used in these essays, however, refer to a narrower definition based on the increase in the number of workers and in the size of the capital stock measured in constant dollar terms. Dennison and Chung in estimating the sources of Japan's 10.04 percent per year growth in the 1953 to 1971 period, for example, attribute 1.14 percent to increases in employment and 2.19 percent to increases in capital.[1] The remaining 6.71 percent is accounted for by increases in hours worked, a more highly educated workforce, improved resource allocation, economies of scale, and advances in knowledge. For China there is no reliable way of measuring these

87

other sources of growth and hence international comparisons at this level of disaggregation are not yet possible. Everything included in Dennison and Chung's 6.71 percent is referred to here as an increase in productivity.

Thus simplified, the difficulties in the way of measuring the contribution of inputs and productivity to China's rising gross national product are no longer insurmountable. Crude estimates of the growth in capital, labor, and net material product (national income according to Chinese definitions) are presented in Table A. To weight the labor and capital inputs, we assume that the share of labor in national income is .7 and that of capital is .3. A higher weight for capital and a lower weight for labor would lower the estimate of productivity growth and vice versa. These weights and growth rates are combined using the equation

$$G_{NMP} = r + W_L G_L + W_K G_K$$

where

$G_{NMP}$ = growth rate of net material product
$r$ = the residual or measure of productivity growth
$W_L$ = the share of labor income in national income
$G_L$ = the growth rate of the labor force
$W_K$ = the share of capital income in national income
$G_K$ = the growth rate of the capital stock

The results of these calculations for the two periods are presented in Table B.

*Appendix*

## Output and Input Growth Rates in China

| Source | 1953–1976 (annual growth rates in percent) | 1977–1984 |
|---|---|---|
| Net material product | | |
| –linked index[a] | 5.7 | 8.8 |
| –1980 prices[b] | 4.4 | 8.3 |
| Labor force[c] | 2.6 | 1.6 |
| Capital stock[d] | 6.5 | 7.2 |

[a]These are the growth rates derived from the national income index at comparable prices given by the Chinese State Statistical Bureau, *Zhongguo tongji nianjian, 1985*, p. 34.

[b]These figures are derived from sectoral figures for national income in current prices. The current price figures for agriculture were deflated using the agricultural purchase price index and those for industry and services were deflated by the index for industrial products prices derived by dividing gross value of industrial output in current prices by gross value of industrial output in 1952, 1957, 1970, and 1980 prices. Since industrial prices changed little over the 1970–84 period, the choice of deflator makes little difference to the outcome of the 1977–84 growth rate, but does influence the 1953–76 rate.

[c]This is the growth rate of the total rural plus urban labor force.

[d]These estimates are based on the figures for fixed capital investment in the 1985 statistical yearbook plus an assumption that the initial capital stock in 1952 was about 100 billion yuan. Neither depreciation nor inventory changes are taken into account although their effects may be offsetting. The resulting growth rate estimates, needless to say, are crude approximations at best. The estimates are actually for 1952–77 and 1978–84, but it has been assumed that growth rates for 1952–76 and 1977–84 would be the same. If the initial capital stock was less than 100 billion yuan, the capital stock growth rates would be slightly higher than those in this table, but not by enough to materially affect the conclusions reached in this analysis. If capital goods prices fell over this period, this would also lead to an underestimate of the capital growth rate, particularly for 1953–76.

*Appendix*

TABLE B

Sources of Growth Calculations for China

| Source | 1953–1976 | 1977–1984 |
|---|---|---|
| Net material product growth rate | 4.4 | 8.3 |
| Contribution of labor | 1.8 | 1.1 |
| Contribution of capital | 1.95 | 2.2 |
| Residual (productivity growth rate) | 0.65 | 5.0 |

# *Notes*

## 1

1. Growth also occurred in parts of Latin America in the period prior to 1950, turning a number of countries in the region into predominantly urban and industrial societies.

2. For those interested in pursuing the economic record of these countries in greater depth, there are a number of general studies available in English including H. Patrick and H. Rosovsky, *Asia's New Giant* (Washington: Brookings, 1976); K. Ohkawa and H. Rosovsky, *Japanese Economic Growth* (Stanford: Stanford University Press, 1973); E. S. Mason, M. J. Kim, D. H. Perkins, K. S. Kim, and D. C. Cole, *The Economic and Social Modernization of the Republic of Korea* (Cambridge: Harvard Council on East Asian Studies, 1980); Samuel P. S. Ho, *Economic Development in Taiwan* (New Haven: Yale University Press, 1978); S. W. Y. Kuo, G. Ranis, and J. C. H. Fei, *The Taiwan Success Story* (Boulder: Westview, 1981), and many other general and more specialized works.

3. Chinese relative prices in the 1950s were skewed in favor of industry and against agriculture, giving a heavier weight to the fast-growing industrial sector in national product. By the late 1970s agricultural prices had risen substantially relative to those of industry, bringing China's relative price structure closer to that of many other developing countries.

4. For a further discussion of education and literacy in pre-modern Japan and China, see R. Dore, *Education in Tokugawa Japan* (London: Routledge and Kegan Paul, 1965) and E. S. Rawski, *Education and Popular Literacy in Ch'ing China* (Ann Arbor: University of Michigan Press, 1979).

5. This statement is based on household surveys done in Korea by the Japanese in the 1930s. See, for example, Chosen Sotokufu, Norin-kyoku, *Noka keizai gaikyo chosa* (1940).

6. These data are from the World Bank, *Accelerated Development in Sub-Saharan Africa* (Washington: World Bank, 1981), p. 181.

7. Leo Orlean, *Professional Manpower and Education in Communist China* (Washington: National Science Foundation, 1961), p. 68.

8. Revenues of government at all levels in Tokugawa Japan may have been over 20 percent of national income although the figure declined in the early Meiji period (E. S. Crawcour, "The Tokugawa Heritage," in *The State and Economic Enterprise in Japan*, ed. W. W. Lockwood (Princeton: Princeton University Press, 1965), p. 31. The Chinese figures are based on Y. C. Wang, *Land Taxation in Imperial China, 1750–1911* (Cambridge: Harvard University Press, 1973).

# Notes

9. See Sang-Chul Suh, *Growth and Structural Change in the Korean Economy, 1910–1940* (Cambridge: Harvard Council on East Asian Studies, 1978).

10. This figure is based on the assumption that per capita income in the early 1950s had recovered to the levels of the 1930s.

11. For a discussion of the nature of the Korean business-government relationship, see L. P. Jones and I. Sakong, *Government, Business and Entrepreneurship in Economic Development: The Korean Case* (Cambridge: Harvard Council on East Asian Studies, 1980).

12. See the appendix for a discussion of the measurement of productivity in East Asia.

13. See, for example, R. I. McKinnon, *Money and Capital in Economic Development* (Washington: Brookings, 1973).

14. Figures for Taiwan's investment and foreign aid are from Council for Economic Planning and Development, *Taiwan Statistical Data Book, 1985*, and those for Korea are from Economic Planning Board, *Major Statistics of Korean Economy, 1982* (1982).

15. The statement made here is based on informed speculation. Confirmation of this view would require interviews of those directly involved in making the key relevant decisions in that period.

16. These figures are from H. Cheney, M. S. Ahluwalia, C. L. G. Bell, J. H. Duloy, and R. Jolly, *Redistribution with Growth* (London: Oxford University Press, 1974), pp. 8–9.

17. Exchange-rate conversions of GNP are a treacherous basis for international comparisons under the best of circumstances, but the problems are particularly severe for China where the exchange rate has only the vaguest relationship to market influences.

18. *The Korea Herald,* November 10, 1985, p. 1.

—

## 2

1. A more systematic account of this period's economic development can be found in D. H. Perkins, "China's Economic Policy and Performance during the Cultural Revolution and Its Aftermath," Development Discussion Paper, no. 161, Harvard Institute for International Development (1984).

2. The World Bank, *China: Socialist Economic Development* (Washington, D.C., 1981), Appendix E, p. 13.

3. A brief methodological note on how productivity change was estimated is contained in the appendix to this volume.

4. This figure is based on a private communication from a Hong Kong businessman.

5. For a detailed discussion of the early struggle over issues of this type

based on field research, see the essays in *Chinese Rural Development: The Great Transformation,* ed. William L. Parish (Armonk: M. E. Sharpe, 1985).

6. See, for example, David Zweig, "Opposition to Change in Rural China: The System of Responsibility and People's Communes," *Asian Survey,* vol. 23, no. 7, July 1983.

7. A useful exposition of Chen Yun's ideas is presented in Nicholas Lardy and Kenneth Lieberthal, *Chen Yun's Strategy for China's Development: A Non-Maoist Alternative* (Armonk: M. E. Sharpe, 1983).

8. Some of the best work currently being done on the industrial reforms is being carried out jointly by the World Bank and the Chinese Academy of Social Sciences. See, for example, William Byrd, Gene Tidrick, Chen Jiyuan, Xu Lu, Tang Zongkun, and Chen Lantong, *Recent Chinese Economic Reforms: Studies of Two Industrial Enterprises,* World Bank Staff Working Papers, no. 652 (Washington, D.C., 1984).

9. *The Korea Herald,* December 27, 1985, p. 8.

10. These figures are from Hollis Chenery and Moshe Syrquin, *Patterns of Development, 1950–1970* (London: Oxford University Press, 1975), p. 50.

11. Chenery and Syrquin, *op. cit.,* p. 55.

12. State Statistical Bureau, *Statistical Yearbook of China: 1984* (Hong Kong: Chinese Information and Agency, 1984), p. 81.

13. State Statistical Bureau, *China: A Statistics Survey in 1985* (Beijing: New World Press, 1985), p. 19.

14. The World Bank, *China: Long Term Issues and Options* (Washington, D.C., 1985), p. 118.

15. *The China Daily,* November 13, 1985.

16. This figure was derived by multiplying 151 yuan, the cost per square meter for residential buildings (urban), times 5.5 square meters per capita, times 330 million people. The cost figure is from State Statistical Bureau, *Statistical Yearbook of China, 1984,* p. 331.

17. Because population growth in the 1950s and 1960s was higher than it is today, the workforce today and for some time into the future will grow faster than the current population growth rate.

18. This term appears to include moving into market towns and the like, but not into cities of 100,000 or more. See, for example, Ren Qingyao, "On the Townization of the Countryside and the Construction of Towns," *Jingji dili,* no. 2, 1985, pp. 146–49.

19. *The China Daily,* November 20, 1985, p. 1

## APPENDIX

1. E. Dennison and W. Chung, "Economic Growth and Its Sources," in H. Patrick and H. Rosovsky, *Asia's New Giant,* p. 94.

# Index

Africa, 9, 13, 14
Agriculture, 45; labor in, 32–33, 73–74; collectivization of, 43, 63; productivity of, 46, 54, 59, 60; reform of, 52–54, 69–70; need to maintain sufficient level of, 59–60; comparable rates of, 77. *See also* Economic growth; People's Communes; "Responsibility system"
Autarky, 5, 22, 43, 50
Automobile: impact of, 34

Black market, 66
Boxer Rebellion, 17

Capital formation: as a percentage of gross domestic product, 8; in South Korea, 8; in Taiwan, 8; in Africa, 9; in China, 9, 41, 46, 48, 57; in Japan, 16
Chen Yun, 62, 67
Chinese Communist party, 41, 63, 80; leadership of, 60–61. *See also* Deng Xiaoping; Mao Zedong
Chinese Politburo, 60–61, 62
Colonialism: effects of, 13, 18
Confucianism, 7, 36; stress on education, 10–11, 41. *See also* Education; Literacy
Consumer society: transition to, 33
Corruption, 63, 64, 67; definition of, 65; in Soviet system, 65; in contrast with personal favors, 65–66
Cultural Revolution, 45, 49

Dai Ichi Bank, 16. *See also* Japan
Daqing oil fields, 46, 50. *See also* Petroleum industry
Deng Xiaoping, 54, 56, 60, 61, 62, 83

East Asia: economic growth of, 4–5, 6, 7–9, 10–14; China's role in, 6; political instability of, 6; pattern of development, 7–9; human resources of, 10, 12, 14, 20; education in, 12; urbanization in, 12–13; outward orientation of, 23, 24, 84; reliance on grain imports, 59–60; mentioned, 3, 7, 36, 48. *See also* Hong Kong; Japan; Singapore; South Korea; Taiwan
Economic growth: income distribution and, 27; sectoral change and, 30; urbanization and, 73
—East Asia: percentage due to capital and labor, 8; percentage due to increased productivity, 8; political stability and, 19–20, 36–37; sources of, 28–29, 84; effect on health, 34
—China: rate of, 9, 43, 48; compared with East Asia, 29–30, 41, 73, 84–85; effects of reform on, 55–56; political support of, 60; impact of, 71–72; 73–74. *See also* Economic policy; Gross national product (GNP)
—Japan: government role in, 15–16, 21–22
—South Korea, 20–21, 22, 25

95

## Index

Economic policy: use of Soviet model, 42–43, 44, 46, 49–50; during 1962–76, 45; reform of, 47–55, 67–71; East Asian pattern of, 56; effects of political change on, 62; problems caused by, 63–67
Education: in East Asia, 10–11, 12, 14; in Africa, 12; in China, 12, 41–42; in Indonesia, 14; in Taiwan, 35. *See also* Literacy
Energy consumption, 51, 57; inefficiency of, 45–46; as compared with India, 46. *See also* Petroleum industry
Enterprise managers, 68, 69
Europe, 4, 5, 51, 59
Exports: Japanese share of, 4; East Asian share of, 4–5; Chinese, 51–52, 58–59. *See also* Economic growth; Gross national product (GNP)

Foreign aid: to Taiwan, 24; to South Korea, 24–25; to China, 42
Foreign direct investment: role of, 24–25; comparable rates of, 24–25; in China, 51
Foreign exchange, 69; amount of, 49; corruption concerning, 66
Friedman, Milton, 20

"Gang of Four," 49
GDP. *See* Gross domestic product
GNP. *See* Gross national product
Government revenues: as compared with Japan, 17
Great Leap Forward, 43–44, 45, 48. *See also* Mao Zedong
Gross domestic product (GDP), 8
Gross national product (GNP), 3, 18–19, 42, 57
—China, 9, 46; compared to South Korea and Taiwan, 30; agriculture and, 32–33, 54; decline of, 45; growth rate of, 45, 48, 56, 71,

72, 75, 84; under Soviet model, 47; discrepancies in, 77; mentioned, 41, 56, 58. *See also* Economic growth; Economic policy
—Hong Kong, 19
—Japan, 3
—Taiwan, 3, 18, 19, 25, 30, 32
—Singapore, 19
—South Korea, 3, 18, 30, 32
"Guest workers," 81

Hong Kong, 3, 7, 13, 35, 36, 37, 51, 84, 85; during colonial period, 18; after 1945, 18–19
Housing, 50, 76, 79–80
Hua Guofeng, 61
Hungary, 56
Hyundai, 20–21. *See also* South Korea

Imperialism, 16
Imports, 49; substitution of, 5, 21, 22; restrictions on, 59
Income: per capita growth of, 72–73, 75; consumption and, 82
Income distribution: political stability and, 27–28; comparable rates of, 28; in China, 29, 42, 57, 63, 64–65; equality of, 35
India, 46
Indo-China, 6
Indonesia, 3, 13–14
Industrial revolution: results of, 4
Industry: inefficiency of, 46–47; reform of, 54–55; concentration of, 78–79
Inflation, 63, 70
International Monetary Fund, 51

Japan: export percentage of, 4; education in, 12; economic growth of, 14–16; political stability of, 15, 16, 35–36; and the United States, 16; outward orientation of, 23; sectoral change in, 32; mentioned, 3, 7, 13, 18, 24,